THE
AWKWARD HUMAN
SURVIVAL GUIDE

HOW TO HANDLE LIFE'S MOST
UNCOMFORTABLE SITUATIONS

BY ADAM DACHIS AND ERICA ELSON

STERLING
New York

CONTENTS

INTRODUCTION

You shouldn't take advice from a book, and that includes this one. Books don't know your life. You're a unique and special person, and a bunch of text can't account for your specific situation. Of course, if you never take advice from a book, you can't put this opening paragraph into practice. Sorry, but we sort of created a paradox. This is awkward.

Let's try this again. You shouldn't take advice from a book, but you can use it as a set of guidelines. Not everything in these pages of embarrassing, uncomfortable situations will apply to you exactly. You can, however, read about some pretty dumb things we've encountered in our lives and the lives of our friends. Use this book as a reminder of the ways in which you can deal with a situation more easily, rather than as religious tome of unbreakable rules.

Advice is always easier said than done. You'll often find yourself in an awkward situation, knowing exactly what you should do but somehow unable to do it. Even when you know you should say something, you'll stare at the person you should say it to, hoping you'll die of natural causes before you have to speak. When a kiss comes your way, and you don't want it, you can't just stick your finger in your date's mouth to stop it instead of honestly confronting your lack of attraction. When you poop in your pants, you can't just sit there and hope the poop will be magically transported into space. You can resolve most awkward situations by confronting them bravely, but you can't just decide to be brave. This book provides infallible advice*, but you can't execute advice like a computer program. You have to make

*It does not, because that's impossible.

mistakes, practice, and learn. Besides, life would be really boring if you did the right thing every time.

We wrote this book because we have a long, long history of screwing up. As you'll discover, we've come to understand the meaning of awkward in ways you've probably never imagined. We've formulated the advice in this book after lots of trial and error. And after enough time and practice, we've found that, whether or not you successfully execute the maneuvers we outline here, enough time and practice will turn your most uncomfortable moments into funny memories. You can wear them like a badge of honor, tell your friends a good story, and move on with your life. You decide whether awkwardness plays a debilitating role or a fun one.

Here's an example: when we moved in together, our apartment came with the dirtiest floors we'd ever seen. The landlord sent someone to clean them, but he didn't do a very good job. We didn't want to pay for a professional housekeeper, so we decided to find a way to get it for free. After a little research on craigslist, we found out that several men like providing free housecleaning services—so long as they get to do it in the nude. The average person would consider a nude cleaner extremely uncomfortable, but thanks to years of stepping out of our comfort zones and handling awkward situations we knew we could manage it. We posted a couple of ads, contacted a few people we found, and eventually settled on a 55-year-old gay man who wanted to clean for straight and bisexual men. A quick phone call set it up and days later he came and made our floors spotless. We don't know exactly what our nude cleaner got out of this experience, but he took pride in his work—as he should. We were very impressed. Initially we wanted to keep this story to ourselves, but we started telling a few people and eventually it spread around the city. First we'd end up at parties and people would ask us to share the experience. Later on, people would tell us the story not knowing where it originated. We could've felt embarrassed and kept our nude cleaner a secret, but we had a lot more fun letting go of the awkwardness and putting it all out there.

Letting go doesn't come naturally. We didn't decide to just take a leap into the world of nude cleaning. We put ourselves through uncomfortable situations until they didn't feel uncomfortable anymore. Through that process, we learned how to handle things better, and you'll find all of that in this book. When you approach awkward situations going forward, you can use that information as a guideline. No single thing we tell you can protect you from awkwardness. Embrace your discomfort and you'll improve your chances of survival.

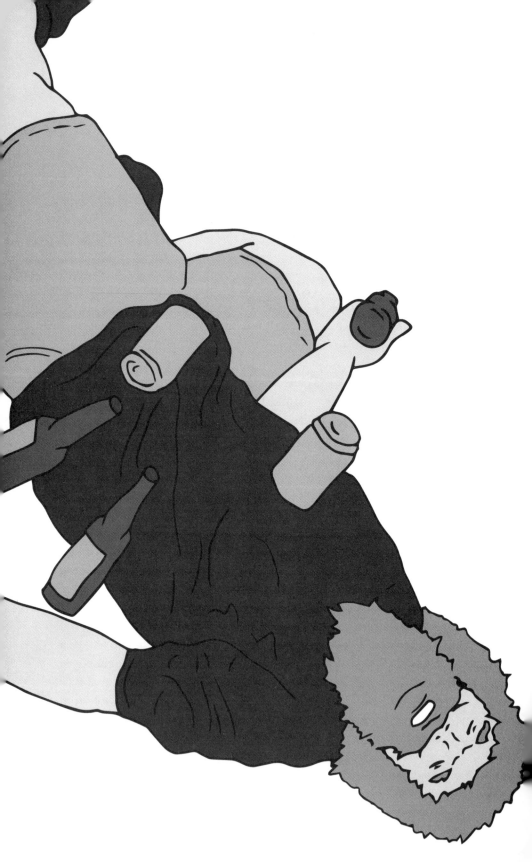

PART I

SOCIAL INTERACTIONS

New social experiences bring all sorts of unexpected things—good and bad. You roll the dice and things might go well, or they might work out terribly. Regardless, they're bound to be a little awkward.

When you encounter any social situation for the first time, you don't really know what to do. Parties create all sorts of complications because you have to learn how to start a conversation and then maintain it without boring your audience to tears. Beyond that, you need to know when to stop, how to get away from people who make you feel uncomfortable, and how to get rid of people who won't leave you alone.

Although there's always the chance of meeting a new and exotic kind of weird person, you might find yourself struggling to have a conversation with someone smarter, dumber, or just different from you. Most social interactions take nothing more than honesty and tact. Those two things intersect less frequently than they should, but it is possible to have kind and truthful conversations—even ones that avoid white lies—without callously trampling over someone else's feelings. Sometimes the truth will hurt. Sometimes you just need to tell people to leave you alone, but if you explain yourself they'll understand. You might make yourself feel bad by stumbling through a conversation, but you can recover by acknowledging your shortcomings and learning from them.

Social interactions take work and require failure. Nobody gets every one of them right, and good social skills don't come naturally. Even people who converse like professionals have acquired their skills by putting themselves out there time and again. When you go out into the world, you can greatly reduce the amount of awkwardness you encounter with a little planning and plenty of practice.

ATTENDING A PARTY WITHOUT BEING SUPER LAME

If you're not a party animal, large gatherings can be an awkward zoo. You can avoid them your whole life, or you can learn how to have a good time.

TT was a shy boy who loved bisexuals and baking. He searched a dating website for bi men, found Ben, and became instantly enamored. After they first chatted online, Ben suggested TT meet him in person for the first time at a party he was throwing that weekend. TT immediately freaked out because he didn't like big groups. He wasn't sure he wanted to go. Ben reassured him, saying that it would be a small party, and that he would introduce him to all his friends. TT seemed satisfied, but an hour before the event, Ben went outside to check the mail. He found a small pan containing a note:

> *Dear Ben. Thank you for inviting me to your party, but I don't think I can come. I feel too nervous. Please accept this cheesecake in my stead. TT*

Ben nearly erupted with pleasure eating the Oreo cheesecake and spent most of the night raving about it to his friends. While TT's choice not to attend the party was understandable, and Ben might have asked too much for a first meet, TT could have had a surprisingly good time if he'd given it a shot.

START WITH THE RIGHT PARTY

There are lots of reasons why people don't like parties. If you're shy or don't know how to make friends, they can be a lot of pressure. Maybe you *don't* want to make new friends and prefer to spend time alone. Or perhaps you're constantly forced into work or family events in which you don't like anyone. Still, every party represents an opportunity to have a great time—if you approach celebrations in the right way. If you want to become comfortable at parties, start with a small one you're more likely to enjoy. If you can have a good time with eight or ten people, you can learn how to navigate a bigger crowd.

Figure out what would make the evening fun for you. Is it about the friends who attend, the food that's served, or the activity? Maybe you don't like keggers, but you enjoy group movie nights, board-game days, or dinner parties. These types of events take away some of the pressure because there is something to do other than stand and talk. Furthermore, there will probably be fewer strangers if it's a small group. If no one you know is hosting this kind of event, take some initiative. Pick an activity you'd like to do or a type of food you want to cook and invite a few friends to join you. If you don't want to take on the responsibility of party planning just yet, ask friends if they can host something at their house and offer to provide food or drinks in exchange.

BRING A FRIEND

Once you're ready to navigate a bigger crowd, having someone to do it with will be a huge help. People who rarely go to parties sometimes challenge themselves by attending events like the office holiday celebration or a friend's graduation. These infrequent gatherings can end up being tough because they don't know a lot of people there and aren't sure who to talk to. In these situations, pick a social friend who you trust and invite him along. It's easier to meet people with a wingman, and if the party ends up being dull, you'll at least have someone to hang out with. Just make sure you don't spend the entire time talking to your buddy, or you'll never meet anyone new.

INFILTRATE

If you've just started at a new school or job, you might not have a wingman yet. However, these kinds of events are made for people to get to know each other better. Find a familiar face from your dorm or office and start up a conversation. If he's not a huge douche, he'll probably be happy to have someone to talk to. If you have a friendly conversation, you can enlist your new acquaintance's help in meeting more people.

> **TRY THIS:** *Do you know a lot of people here? I just started at this job/ school and haven't met anyone yet.*
> **OR THIS:** *I'm going to try mingling a little. Do you want to make the rounds with me?*

Of course, you don't want to spend the entire night with the first person you speak to. Once you've said hi to a familiar face, try it with someone you've never seen before. If no one is standing alone, walk up to a group. This may feel uncomfortable at first, since you're joining a conversation you know nothing about. Keep in mind that it's a party—if these people wanted it to be a private conversation, they would have it elsewhere. Ask a question about what's being discussed, mention a shared interest, or compliment someone on the point he just made. Pretty soon you'll be part of the conversation. If you don't feel confident being that bold, pretend. Treat the night as an acting exercise in which you pretend to be an extrovert. Confidence is a huge asset in becoming a more social person, and this is a case in which you can fake it 'til you make it. If you put in the time and effort, it should become much easier to talk to strangers without worrying you'll embarrass yourself.

BRING SOME STORIES

There is often that person at a party that everyone crowds around listening to. If you want to make new friends or find a date when you go to a party, it helps to make yourself as interesting as possible. Instead of simply asking questions or making small talk when you meet someone, share a unique story. This will, at the very least, make you memorable. Try to work the story into the conversation—don't just walk up to a person and start talking about your great aunt's funeral. Once you've shared a weird story, others will feel encouraged to do so, and the conversation will become more fun. Ben understood TT's shyness because he used to be the same way. As Ben grew up, he forced himself to attend more social events and share weird personal facts. Now Ben attends parties at which people he doesn't even know have heard his stories through the grapevine.

DRINK THE RIGHT AMOUNT

Having a couple beers might open you up and make it easier to talk to people. In fact, it could be a good idea for you to hit the bar before you dive into the crowd. However, don't go overboard with your drinking in an attempt to feel more comfortable. You don't want to be remembered as the guest who threw up on the dog because you were too drunk.

Learning to socialize is like any other skill. It takes time, practice, and a little help from your friends. While you may never love spending time with large groups of people, you can learn to feel comfortable attending most parties.

GETTING OUT OF WEIRD CONVERSATIONS

Talking to people can be great, but sometimes you don't really care about what they're saying. You can politely listen to an extent, but there are some conversations you should take care to exit before you want to gouge out your own eyes in frustration.

Raymond was a hypochondriac who worked at the DMV. Twenty years of government service had worn him down, and he was often distracted when filing paperwork. This was the case when Claire went to renew her registration. Moments after starting the process, he looked up at the ceiling and asked Claire whether she had energy-saving light bulbs in her home. He was concerned because they contained mercury, and his neighbor had just had a heart attack. He suspected it was due to mercury poisoning because of something he'd been through himself.

Raymond used to have metal tooth fillings, which slowly released mercury into his veins. The tingling and numbness in his arms became so unbearable that Raymond changed all his fillings to composite resin. While this removed the mercury poisoning, Raymond believed the composite resin increased estrogen production due to the chemicals inside slowly seeping into his mouth. He was convinced it was affecting his look and behavior. As Claire waited for Raymond to process her paperwork, he asked her if he looked like a woman, and if it would be worth becoming a transsexual. She didn't feel qualified to answer but continued talking to him because she didn't want to risk losing her registration paperwork. The lesson here is to remove yourself from an uncomfortable conversation before you advise a stranger on sex change options.

BE CLEAR

Sometimes the conversation is uncomfortable because it's really boring, or you're making small talk with a person you don't really like. There are a few ways to get out of there without being offensive. If you're at a party, excusing yourself to get a drink or to say hi to someone will work with most people. If you're worried about the person following you, try saying something like, "It's been nice talking to you. I'm going to go make the rounds." This puts a definite end to the conversation. If you're alone with someone or you're conversing over the phone, you can say something like, "I'd love to catch up, but I have somewhere to be" or "I'm sorry, but I can't talk right now." Using words like *have to* and *can't* make it clear that you want the conversation to end.

POINT TO THE PROBLEM

If you were having a nice conversation until someone said something that made you uncomfortable, you don't necessarily need to end it. Specify your issue. A person might offend you with what he thinks is a benign joke and have no idea. If you're uncomfortable with the topic as a whole, you can suggest changing the subject to something lighter or saying you'd rather not argue over a political or religious issue. Claire could have said, "Thank you for warning me about the mercury, but I'd really just like to get my registration in order." Most people will be fine with changing the subject once they realize you're not okay with it. If you're afraid of offending a boss or another authority figure, you can make light of the situation. For example, "We're at a party, no one wants to talk politics!" or "I don't necessarily need to know the intricate details of your sex life, Joe." People are often less offended by a joke than a direct request.

If someone isn't taking normal social cues and won't let you exit the conversation, you'll have to be more direct with him. "I don't want to talk about this anymore," or "I'm going to leave if we don't move on from this" may seem harsh but will save you time and energy.

Just because you start a conversation doesn't mean you have to stay in it forever. Speak up before you fall asleep and get out of there if you need to.

OPTING OUT OF ACTIVITIES YOU CAN'T AFFORD

Once you hit adulthood, you have to handle a lot of expenses. Rent, bills, food, student loans, and car payments add up quickly. It will only get worse as you grow older and have kids or adopt a variety of reptiles. You'll be lucky if you have some change left over and you should get to choose how you spend that money. While it can be hard to say no to a friend, declining things that exceed your budget will help you stay out of debt.

Claire and Ben met in a college class about pornography and became life-long friends. Ben discovered a delicious dumpling establishment and invited Claire to come along. She couldn't afford it so he brought his long-time girl-friend, Josephine. Josephine was on the South Beach diet and couldn't eat any carbs, so she would suck the meat and broth out of the juicy pork dump-lings and give Ben the remaining skins. Since Ben was a vegetarian who loved carbs, this worked out well. After Josephine dumped him, he decided to eat his way to recovery. Claire agreed to go to the dumpling restaurant with him once for moral support. As Claire sucked the meat out of the dump-lings for her friend, she realized just how delicious they were.

She became addicted to the excellent food: the spicy noodles, the garlic green beans, the fried rice. Each dinner cost close to $30, but she couldn't stop going. Claire found herself using all her disposable income on dump-lings. She cancelled her cable, started cutting her own hair, and sold some of her clothes. Ben was still sad about Josephine, and Claire didn't want to tell him that their dumpling outings had become a financial burden. One month she realized she couldn't buy her mom a birthday gift because she barely had enough in her account to pay her power bill. She swallowed her pride with her pork buns and admitted the truth to Ben: she couldn't afford to go out as often as he did and needed to be more careful with her money.

BE PICKY

If you buy a jaguar and then you tell your friend you can't go out for her birthday because you ran out of money, you might seem like a jerk. However, if you're a broke student who is always careful with your money and your friend wants to make you pay for a $150 dinner, he's the jerk. Choose the things to spend your extra cash on wisely, and don't feel obligated to go to an expensive event because all your friends will be in attendance. You can choose to save your money for classes, medical expenses, or bird supplies. Just phrase it in a way that doesn't make your friend feel like he doesn't matter to you.

> **BAD:** *I'm going to skip your party because it's too expensive.*
> **GOOD:** *I wish I could go to your birthday party, but things are a little tight this month. Why don't you come over next week and we can make dinner and celebrate together?*

Planning ahead can help you miss fewer things. If you know you always go broke after the weekend because you go out drinking, put aside a portion of your paycheck on Thursday or Friday. That way, if a friend comes in from out of town or you have to get someone an unexpected gift, you'll have a little pile to draw from. If you still have it at the end of the month, you can go out and barhop to your heart's content. You can also tell your friends or family that they need to tell you ahead of time if they expect you to show up to something that costs money. While some people can fly home for a Bark Mitzvah* or an anniversary party whenever they want, others need to be more selective. Planning a trip will be much easier with a larger window.

SUGGEST AN ALTERNATIVE

Society puts a lot of pressure on us to spend money. Men often feel like they need to pay for their date and end up buying dinner at a restaurant they can't afford. Parents sometimes pay for an expensive wedding to show everyone

---

a Bar Mitzvah for a dog.

how important their daughter is. Friends spend a bunch of money on each other at Christmas when they might need the cash for more crucial expenses. Some payments you can't get out of, but regarding social activities you can often suggest a comparable activity that costs much less.

If you want to impress your date, cook dinner at home instead of going out. If you want to watch a movie, download it from iTunes or Amazon instead of going to the theater. Find homemade gifts to make for the holidays. If you have to go to a certain event, you can always offer to trade a service for an expense. This doesn't mean you should whore yourself out to your friends. For instance, you can say you'll be the designated driver if everyone splits the cost of your cover at a club. When your friends plan an expensive night out, you can mention that you'd like to go but the activity is outside your price range. If they don't change their plans to accommodate you, they'll at least know for the future that you need to be frugal with your spending.

If the event is something important like a wedding, you can talk to the bride or groom about ways to make it work. A lot of people will skip far-away marriages because of the costs involved: a plane ticket, a hotel, a gift, an outfit. You might be able to stay with a family member or use someone's frequent flier miles to buy your flight. If you can remove some of the big expenses, you'll be able to go without completely breaking the bank. Instead of feeling embarrassed about your lack of funds, show your friends that you care by finding out if there's a way for you to be there.

BORING IS BETTER THAN BROKE

Be realistic about traveling, buying gifts, and going out. There will be periods of your life when you literally don't have an extra dime. Be honest if you can't afford to go out with friends for a few months. There's a difference between being cheap and being worried about paying your rent. As an adult, you may feel shame when you reveal that you can't afford something. However, going into a huge amount of debt because you spent your money irresponsibly will be far more embarrassing. Most people will respect your candor and understand the situation. If they don't, they probably shouldn't be part of your life.

People who make a comfortable salary may not understand how quickly small expenses add up for you. Ben hadn't even considered that dining out encumbered Claire. Don't be a dick by making them feel bad for not having more money. Just explain what you can and can't afford and suggest activities that work for you. Decent human beings will find a compromise that works for everyone.

MANAGING PEOPLE WITH NO BOUNDARIES

Most humans have a sixth sense that allows us to see these invisible things called boundaries. Said boundaries prevent us from taking a dump on our co-worker's desk, stealing our neighbor's collection of decorative spoons, or throwing bagels at innocent passersby. Not all people possess the ability to see the difference between appropriate and inappropriate behaviors, but a little coaching can teach them all they need to know.

Ben got a job just out of college at a tech startup with a business-casual environment. His former classmate and friend Arlo lived at home with his parents and spent most of his days only eating, pooping, and downloading seventies-era glamour shots of Lynda Carter. After a messy breakup with Samantha, his girlfriend of two years, he sent Ben an email titled, "Does this look like her?" While in a meeting, with his computer visible to the crowd, Ben opened it. Inside he found a picture of a naked woman, reminiscent of Samantha, using a spatula for a decidedly sexual purpose. Ben quickly grabbed the computer and threw it across the room. Nobody saw the pornography. Well, no one other than his boss.

Arlo rarely thought through the impact of his actions. He'd proposition women in a park while they played with their children. He'd call his friends repeatedly and leave messages about his impending suicide just so they would call him back. Arlo worked at a fast food establishment and his daily routine included saving at least one mostly-beef patty to mail to PETA at the end of the workday. He didn't fully comprehend the ramifications of his behavior. He only imagined the immediate effects of everything he did, acting completely on impulse and obliterating boundaries at every turn. Still, while this kind of person may seem hopeless, a little guidance often does the trick.

THERE IS NO SUCH THING AS COMMON SENSE

We often regard our own boundaries as common sense and fail to understand how others don't automatically know when they've acted inappropriately. When it comes to behavior, you should always assume that you are the only one who knows the rules in your head. If you consider common sense—the behavioral rules we ought to discover naturally through prolonged existence—it's kind of ridiculous. Common sense can't exist.

Sure, most of us know in a general sense that we shouldn't kill other people, but you'll find plenty of disagreement on that point when it comes to, for example, capital punishment. A lot of people would execute a terrorist, or feel rapists deserve death rather than rehabilitation. If you put a group of people in a room—even if they grew up in the same home—they'll disagree on a variety of subjects when the details come into play. So how can you have common sense when all humanity can't even agree on something as simple as murder? You can't, and so you shouldn't ever expect anyone to respect your boundaries if you never make them known—regardless of how obvious they may seem to you.

EXPLAIN THE RULES OF YOUR WORLD

When Arlo sent porn to Ben's work email, he couldn't have known Ben would open it in a meeting. Nevertheless, most of us know not to send inappropriate imagery to the office because doing so creates so many opportunities for a problem. While common sense might dictate that Arlo should have known to share the photo another way—or not at all—he'd never spent any time in an office and had no context for the issue such an email could cause.

You should never assume someone understands the rules of your world. Instead, look out for signs that point to this fact. Hopefully said signs won't include an embarrassing moment for you, but regardless you need to use them as teachable moments. Relationship and family therapist Roger S. Gil explains how best to approach the problem:

Boundary declarations are best made with clear statements that iden-

tify which behaviors are "too far," communicate how they make you feel, state what behavior changes you would like to see, and what course of action you'll have to take if the behavior persists.

For example, "Tom, I know you're only joking when you talk about my mother's morbid obesity, but I seriously don't like it when you do it, so please stop or else I'm going to have to back off."

Most friends will apologize when they breach a boundary. We all have them and we all overstep from time to time because our boundaries vary. If your friend cares about you, he will feel bad if he hurts you. So long as you don't put forward any accusations and, rather, explain how their behavior affects you, they shouldn't want to continue acting that way. Maturity levels will dictate how quickly friends learn your boundaries, so don't expect immediate changes in everyone. If someone important to you needs a little more effort, stay patient and give him a chance to adjust. While we can't have common sense, we can have our own common behaviors. Changing them takes more work than pointing out the problem, so don't discount the effort of a boundary-breaching friend.

GETTING RID OF PEOPLE WHO WON'T LEAVE

Even your closest friends can become a burden when they overstay their welcome. Most people will realize when it's time to go, but others require further instruction.

Olive and Tessa went out for drinks to celebrate the end of finals. Since Olive didn't want to drive, she asked Tessa if she could stay at her place in the city. Tessa had asked her to leave before the family dinner she was hosting the next day. However, Olive had a terrible hangover and insisted on staying the whole weekend, alternately puking and demanding water with lemon, low-sodium crackers, and free-range chicken broth. When Olive could use her mouth to speak, she didn't bother to utter an apology, a thank-you, or anything but demands to Tessa. Tessa complied because she felt bad for Olive, but she went too far. Friends don't have a right to your servitude, so don't let someone overstay his welcome just because it seems like the right thing to do.

FIGURE OUT AN EXIT STRATEGY

If you often find yourself wishing people would just leave your house already, you may need to pre-plan a little. Set a specific end time when you invite people to a dinner party. If you've already mentioned that you have to be up for work the next day, they'll understand why you want them to go. Whether you want to spend time with your kids, get some work done, or exercise, you can remind them that you need to get started on that activity. If a friend from out of town asks to stay with you, decide how long you'll want him to stay. While there are some people you might be able to live with for a few weeks, you probably have friends who'd get on your nerves after a couple days.

> **BAD:** *Of course you can stay with me while you're in town.*
> **GOOD:** *I'd love to have you stay with me for the weekend.*
> **GOOD:** *Monday through Thursday would be the best days for me to host you.*

If your friends don't leave when they are supposed to, it's totally acceptable to remind them that you need the house back to yourself.

GET THE MESSAGE ACROSS

There are a few direct but polite ways to get people to go. Think of it like ending a phone conversation. Most of us wouldn't feel bad saying we need to hang up, and there's no reason not to act the same way in person.

> **TRY THIS:** *It's been great having you over but I have to get back to work.*
> **OR THIS:** *I hate to be a party pooper but I'm tired and I need to call it a night.*

This way, you're expressing regret and offering a logical explanation for why they have to go.

BE FIRM WHEN NEEDED

If you're dealing with people who don't recognize normal social cues, you'll have to give them a direct order like, "I need you to go home." If the other ways haven't worked, you should be less worried about offending them and more interested in getting them to depart. If it's a houseguest or someone who's between apartments, you can offer to help in other ways. Suggest another friend who they could stay with for awhile or offer to visit rental units with them. Make it clear that you're doing this to help get them out of your house.

Some people will take advantage of your hospitality any chance they get. Other people just don't pick up on your desire for them to leave. Be polite but clear when you want someone to go.

PART II

DEALING WITH SOCIETY

Most people suck. We even struggle to interact with the people we like from time to time. It's hard to understand that a stranger might be more than just some asshole who cut you off at a turn or purchased the last double chocolate cupcake you stood in line for twenty minutes to buy. Our brains like to judge people—especially people who cut you off in traffic—so when you encounter a new person, you have a pretty good chance of hating her guts. As civilized people, however, we have to make an effort to bury that discomfort and move past it into empathy.

When out and about in the world, people will push you and not care, steal your parking spots, talk loudly during a movie, and do a number of other things to break the many tiny social contracts we like to believe exist. On one hand, we should consider ourselves lucky. Someone may have just stolen our parking spot but better that than our flat-screen TV. On the other hand, these minor infractions cause us grief. We wonder whether or not to confront transgressors, and how to go about it if we do. You don't want to let the jerks of the world run around and do whatever they please, but you can't pick every battle and expect to win—or even feel like you did the right thing.

Society forces a number of awkward confrontations upon us because we judge too quickly, care too much about the day's minutiae, and fight battles better left un-fought. Still, sometimes we need to stand up for ourselves and kick society in the balls. The awkwardness dissolves once you learn to walk on that fine line.

DEALING WITH NOISY NEIGHBORS

We don't live in a silent void. We live with people. Unfortunately, some people operate at a higher volume than others. If you tell them to quiet down incorrectly, you run the risk of becoming a jerk they don't care to help. And then the noise doesn't stop. And you don't sleep. When your neighbors make too much noise, you have to approach the situation with care, or the problem will continue.

When Jeanette woke up each morning, normally in a drunken stupor, she would drape a few inches of fabric over her skeletal frame and leave for a day of adventure. Upon returning thirty minutes later with a Frappuccino, she would then pass out in front of the television until the late afternoon. Jeanette would wake only when her boyfriend stopped by. After he would make love to her gently, she'd question his sexuality loud enough for the entire neighborhood to hear, and then crank up the music and dance the night—and her troubles—away. She would repeat the process again the following morning. In short, she was an ideal neighbor.

Ben lived in the apartment adjacent to Jeanette. He was not a huge fan of the six-hour dubstep mix called "Do Me Like a Man or Get Out" that comprised Jeanette's waking hours. He left polite notes on Jeanette's door and contacted the landlord, but avoided any kind of direct confrontation. While a simple note can sometimes resolve an issue, neighbors don't feel bad for pieces of paper. Paper doesn't have a tired face neighbors can see due to lack of sleep caused by loud sex. Had Ben worked up the confidence to visit his neighbor and ask for a polite resolution, he might have received a change in soundtrack.

DON'T BE A WIMP

You can't always know whether you live next to Jeanette, the dark lord Satan, or a perfectly reasonable human being. Some people make noise and just have no idea. You might wake up angry one night when you hear music blasting through your walls, but until you've expressed your concern in person, you must give your neighbor the benefit of the doubt. If she meets you for the first time and you breathe fire in her face, you will look like the bad guy—not her.

If you can't stand the noise, head over to the offender's apartment. Before you go, build up the necessary courage for a confrontation or calm down—whatever your mood deems necessary. Knock on the door, say hello, and politely ask for a little more quiet. Feel free to mix in some subtextual guilt.

> **DON'T DO THIS:** *Can you turn off your music? It's late, you shouldn't be playing it at this hour, and I'm trying to sleep.*
> **DO THIS:** *Your music woke me up, and I have to get up early for work tomorrow. Can we figure out a volume that works for both of us, and some quiet hours so the music doesn't wake anybody up?*

You want to avoid judgment of noisy neighbors. First of all, they may not know they've upset you. Second, and regardless, if you go into angry asshole mode, they will go into angry asshole mode. No matter how justified a complaint, when it's barked at other people just after you meet them, you'll seem wrong. Just as lawyers advise their clients before they take the witness stand, advise yourself to stay calm and collected. Anger makes you look crazy. If the other people get angry and you stay calm, they seem even crazier. In the end, you'll always win by playing it cool.

CREATE AN INCONVENIENCE

When your personal efforts fail, and you simply live next door to an inconsiderate jerk, you should involve people of authority. First, check your lease for any mention of quiet hours. Many landlords make their tenants agree to keep the volume down from 11:00 PM to 8:00 AM, if not for an even longer period, and you have the right to complain if your neighbor violates this rule. Put your complaint into writing—digitally or otherwise—and send it to your landlord. For example:

> Dear Landlord,
>
> My neighbor in unit #2 wakes me up most nights with loud music and other noises. I've politely asked her to make less noise in the evenings so my roommate can study. Although she agreed, she hasn't made any adjustments. Per section 5.7 in my lease, quiet hours are between 11:00 PM and 8:00 AM. I would greatly appreciate it if you could speak with her and let her know she cannot continue to disturb others in the building during these hours. You can reach me via email or at 323-555-5555 with any questions or updates.
>
> Thank you,
> Ben

A good landlord will speak to their noisy tenants and let them know they've violated their lease. Hopefully, their behavior will change. In the event it does not, and your landlord won't help any further, you can also involve the police. Any time you hear a disturbance, call the police and report it. When your neighbors make too much noise, they inconvenience you. You want to turn the tables and make their actions inconvenient for them. If you force them to deal with the police every single time they wake you up, they will stop waking you up. Remember: don't contact the police unless you've exhausted all other options. Most neighbors listen to reason and a simple conversation will resolve the issue.

Don't forget to forgive, either. Most of us cause disturbances sometimes. People make noise and don't know what others hear. Think about how embarrassed you'd feel if you screamed a few choice things in the throes of passion and later found out that the entire neighborhood heard it. We often miscalculate how much privacy our walls afford, so don't go crazy over an infraction or two. Save the extreme measures for the Jeanettes of the world, who share their misery with everyone through emasculating dubstep sexcapades.

COMPLAINING ABOUT FOOD AT A RESTAURANT

There's a menu reserved for select restaurant patrons that features exotic ingredients, startling flavor combinations, and dishes tailor-made for each diner. How do you become a member of the elite? You complain about your food.

James worked as a chef in a family-style restaurant in a small midwestern city. When customers issued a mean or ridiculous complaint, the wait staff brought the food back to the kitchen to supposedly fix the problem. Instead, they called upon a variety of specialty recipes to "enhance" the food with their bodies and bodily fluids. For example, to reward a guest for blowing up over what he perceived to be a mediocre plate of pasta, one of the female chefs took the noodles into the bathroom, massaged them on (and supposedly in) her genitals, and asked the scorned waiter to serve them back to the whining diner. In most cases, no one said a word.

When you complain and your food tastes a little off when it comes back, the only thing worse than imagining why is knowing why. In the end, nobody wins with a big bowl of genital-flavored pasta. The restaurant likely loses a customer, and that customer leaves with a bad taste in his or her mouth. Fortunately, you can avoid horrible scenarios like this if you complain effectively.

THE CUSTOMER IS ALWAYS WRONG

You don't have to suffer through a bad meal due to a perverse need for politeness or fear of the kitchen staff depositing bodily fluids into your food. You only need to swallow your pride and assume you could be wrong. You may order a hamburger well done and receive a menstruating beef patty, but errors in communication happen to everyone. Perhaps you gave an unclear order, the waiter misheard what you said, or the kitchen simply made a mistake and your waiter didn't know. Eugene once sent a burger back because he found dandruff on it, only to later discover it came from his own head. If you don't want your food marinated in urine—or worse—your best bet is to keep an open mind.

Approach the situation with no bias. For example, you can say the following when you receive undercooked food:

I know this isn't your fault, but my food is undercooked.

We spoke to a number of waiters who preferred this method because it gets the message across quickly without blaming anyone. They told us patrons often cause errors by neglecting to read the menu, but it doesn't hurt to be polite even when someone else makes the mistake.

When the waiter can't solve the problem, ask for a manager. So long as you do not request anything ridiculous and remain respectful, most establishments will accommodate your needs or even comp your meal. Because free dining beats a meal saturated in vaginal discharge, kindness over anger is always best when sending food back at a restaurant.

TELLING SOMEONE HE PARKS LIKE AN ASSHOLE

If you need evidence of evolution, just take a look at the modern asshole. The once-simple poop-dispensing orifice developed limbs, a torso, a brain, and can now operate motor vehicles. The species looks and acts like humans, so you may go about your day without noticing the many assholes in your midst.

Helen was a tiny woman with a tiny vagina. At a recent genital waxing, the aesthetician—lacking the requisite jeweler's magnifying glass—miscalculated and ripped off a strip of skin on Helen's nether regions. Helen stopped at her local pharmacy to pick up a bottle of painkillers and an ice pack, thinking more of her torn labia than her terrible parking job. When she returned, she noticed two things: she'd parked in two spots and a teen-age boy thought it wise to let her know by keying that information into her car door. Helen summoned her flair for the dramatic and swung her bag at the boy's head. He turned around and punched her in the face. Upon real-izing he'd punched a girl and unsure of what to do about it, he just ran. Helen picked herself up from the ground and opened her car door with an unfin-ished message that read "THIS BITCH NEEDS TWO." Through all the com-motion, the irony was lost on her.

PICK YOUR BATTLES

Some people, regardless of the size or state of their vagina, have bad days. They may drive and park selfishly or poorly. You can think of these people as temporary assholes. Many others, however, work very hard to maintain asshole status throughout the course of their lives. Few people can distinguish between these two classifications when driving and no one can tell their parking techniques apart. Although we may drive and park properly in order to accommodate the other humans around us, we've all made mistakes on the road. Most of the time, when someone cuts you off or uses more than his share of parking spots, you need to just let it go.

When you give someone grief, whether in person or by note, you run the risk of becoming the asshole yourself. Perhaps he had a terrible day, and then you wrote a note to say he parks like an asshole. Yes, he inconvenienced you and possibly others, but you have nothing to gain by sharing your anger. Even a seemingly polite note can come across as cruel because the recipient will assume an irritated undertone. You can justify your frustration all you want, but your note will most likely serve to make the parker feel bad, and it won't solve the problem. Lifelong assholes won't change, because that's part of their nature. Temporary assholes will just feel hurt. Only you will feel a mild amount of relief, and that's not enough to justify fighting a stupid, point-less battle that won't make a difference in your life.

Of course, no rule comes without an exception. When you have to deal with the same asshole repeatedly, you should leave a note. If you can talk to him in person, even better. Much like a noisy neighbor, many people don't realize they cause a problem until someone points it out. If you can do this politely and leave your anger out of it, you can make progress. If you have to leave a note because you don't know the owner of the car, write it as gently as possible.

DON'T DO THIS: *Please don't park your car in both spots. You make it impossible for me to park and that's very frustrating.*
DO THIS: *I own/rent the parking spot next to yours and I often can't get in because you park over the line. I don't know if you know you're doing this, but it would be really helpful if you could leave a little more room for me. Thanks!*

You might think the first (bad) example seems fine. If you said that out loud, with a polite tone, you could seem to make a reasonable request. As mentioned earlier, however, you'll sound like a jerk in the mind of the ass-hole parker. It helps to exaggerate your politeness to make it difficult for the recipient to read your note in any other way. When you have to leave a note, make sure you leave a nice one. You won't get what you want when you get mad.

DEALING WITH OBNOXIOUS AIRPLANE PASSENGERS

You make the drive to the airport, pay at least $25 to check a bag, take your carry-ons up through security, unpack them, go through a low-level x-ray machine, get felt up by a stranger, repack your bag, and wait nervously to board a plane you'll wish you never boarded after you get stuck on the tarmac for an hour or two. When we put ourselves through the process of flying, it's easy to overlook the small miracle that most of us get to our destination still sane and unscathed. However, some people will lose their shit, and you'll have to deal with it.

Ben found himself on a cross-country flight seated behind Gary, a difficult passenger and aneurysm waiting to happen. After Ben placed his airline-approved carry-on backpack under the seat, Gary angrily jabbed it with his heels, indicating that it was impinging upon his territory. He stood up, turned to Ben, and screamed, "I WILL NOT BE TREATED LIKE CATTLE!" Rather than just asking if Ben could move the bag, Gary yelled until a flight attendant took the offending backpack and put it in the overhead bin.

Ben didn't like this. He had done nothing wrong, while Gary got what he wanted by throwing a temper tantrum. With a long flight ahead, Ben decided to seek his revenge. He scanned the plane for opportunities and realized one was seated right beside him: the father of a small, annoying child seated in another row. Ben asked the father if his kid would like to sit next to him so they could be together and the father happily agreed. For the rest of the flight, the child screamed and kicked the seat in front of him. When Gary protested, he got nowhere. An angry man couldn't win a fight against an always-innocent child.

Unfortunately, few flights provide easily relocatable disobedient minors for the purpose of revenge. Nevertheless, you can deal with an asshole passenger in a variety of clever ways.

GET AWAY FROM THE JERK

We can only fight so many battles, and picking one with a random asshole on a plane generally won't turn out for the best. Before you turn your flight into a revenge plot, consider how you can find a new seat.

If a flight has a number of open, standard coach seats, you can request a change and usually get it. For the most part, the flight crew doesn't care where you sit so long as the airline doesn't lose money by moving you there. If you want a different seat, ask for it. When you see an open seat, sometimes you can just switch to it without an issue. Try to do this before the boarding door closes, however, or you might seem obvious. If you get caught, you'll have to explain your situation and you might get moved back to where you started.

As demonstrated by Ben and Gary, complaints go a long way on an airplane. Content and accuracy don't matter—the flight crew just wants you to shut up and sit down because that makes the trip go by more smoothly for everyone. That said, don't resort to anger if you don't need to. A calm demeanor makes any complaint reasonable. For example, find the flight crew in the back of the plane and ask for their help with a sensitive issue concerning the asshole passenger you want to get away from. You can say something like this:

> *Sorry to bother you, but I have a sort of uncomfortable situation with the passenger in front of me. I'm not sure if he has some sort of medical issue, but he's been farting the entire flight and I have a very sensitive nose. Would it be possible to move to another seat, or could you talk to him about it?*

You can make up any virtually harmless story you like, but try to keep the topic to something a flight attendant won't want to deal with. Giving them the option of talking to the passenger about something embarrassing allows them to think about actually doing that. Nobody wants to have an awkward conversation with a passenger about his farting problem, so you can expect the flight crew will move you to a new seat if at all possible. If you can't, and you want your revenge, read on.

STOP AN ASSHOLE FROM RECLINING

When you wind up with a jerk in front of you, stop his or her seat from reclining with a water bottle. Simply lower your tray, jam a water bottle between it and the locking mechanism, and it'll prevent a seat from reclining. That means a little revenge and added comfort for you. If the asshole notices, you can easily get yourself out of trouble. Just claim it was an accident and move on.

TAKE FREQUENT TRIPS TO THE BATHROOM

If you end up seated next to the asshole passenger and can cross his or her path by getting out of your seat, do it as often as possible. You have the right to pee and poop, so exercise that right frequently. He or she will not enjoy a regularly interrupted flight but can't prevent you from doing your business. For added effect, talk about your overactive bladder and/or your irritable bowel syndrome each time you leave. When you get a jerk seated in front of you, just bump their seat each time you get up.

Note: Don't use this tactic if you interrupt the flight of an innocent passenger in the process. Revenge makes you enough of an asshole already, so don't bother others.

JUST LET IT GO

In the end, do you really make the world better by ruining someone's day even more? He won't learn a lesson from your revenge, and you won't feel much better if you spend most of your flight irritating an asshole. Perfect flights rarely happen and you can't always avoid a crappy experience. You can let go of your flight rage and just try to enjoy the time you have.

PART III

FRIENDS AND ACQUAINTANCES

When it comes to people you've never met, you have nothing to lose. Friends change that. When you make friends, suddenly everyone around you seems to be asking for favors, confronting problems, and sharing secrets—all activities that pose a risk of awkwardness. If we avoid that risk, we can spend more time reaping the benefits of friendship: comfort, entertainment, stability. However, when you circumvent these situations instead of confronting them, that leaves a lot unsaid and unresolved, and that in itself is awkward.

Friendships can survive a lot, but when we fail to deal with a problem, there's a chance that it could blow up into a huge fight. What doesn't really matter much to our friends can seem like a huge issue to us, so we keep it to ourselves, let it fester, and then explode in anger. Friendships survive big arguments far less often than they survive the calm discussion of a little gripe. We run ourselves in circles trying to avoid the awkwardness we think might hurt our relationships with others. Ultimately, we just need to get out of our heads.

Just as we aim for tact and honesty in general social situations, we need to do the same with our friends. We make ourselves a little vulnerable by doing so, but friendships grow when two people feel they can trust each other with deeper and deeper truths. Of course, some friends turn out to suck, and you can't avoid every unpleasant situation. You can lead by example, however, and handle the downsides gracefully.

ASKING FOR A FAVOR

Most people suck at asking for favors because they fear a negative answer. As a result, they waffle around the subject and end up wasting everyone's time. If you need something, you just need to ask.

Claire always dreamed of writing for a television program. She moved to Los Angeles, made a few contacts, and decided to ask one for advice. Claire actually wrote a great letter, but first let's take a look at how she could've failed:

Dear James,

This is Claire Baker; how are you? We haven't talked in a long time and I wanted to say hello to reconnect. I also heard you have a new show in the works and I happen to be looking for work. I'd love a job if you've got one.

I've been working on all sorts of things since I moved to LA. I wrote this one movie called Mrs. Frumpterly's Kitchen. It's like Mrs. Doubtfire, but with Ricky Gervais and cooking. And he accidentally poisons his kids by cooking so that's why his wife wants a divorce. I also wrote another one called Kung Bao, which is like the Karate Kid but with Chinese cooking. I know it sounds like it might be a little racist but it's not! I think you'd really like them, and I could send you them so you could read them and tell me what you think.

Hope to hear from you soon!

Claire

While the beginning of this letter might seem innocuous, every sentence points to a different mistake. After that, it just gets much worse. When you ask for help, you need to get to the point, know when to stop talking (or writing), avoid desperation, and use a little creativity.

ASK FIRST, COMPLIMENT LATER

When you ask for a favor, ask first. You might feel like you should begin your request with a series of niceties, but that makes you seem duplicitous. Step into your recipient's shoes: if someone you haven't heard from in awhile suddenly showed an interest in your life and made you feel appreciated, only to ask for a favor after five minutes of building you up, you'd feel cheated. What seems genuine in the beginning becomes insincere upon revealing an ulterior motive. The simple solution? Reverse the order.

Rather than talking people up before making a request, just make the request. Afterward, you can ask about them and their life. That way your intentions are clear and you won't make the rest of the conversation ring false.

KNOW WHEN TO SHUT UP

When you ask a close friend for a favor you don't have to worry too much about the length of your request. When you ask a stranger, acquaintance, or even a friend you don't see often, consider his time. Figure out what you want and how to explain it quickly. When you want something from someone else, keep your request concise. It shows that you value his time, know what you want, and know how to ask for it. You can always provide additional details later.

TRY A CREATIVE APPROACH

Sometimes you need a favor from people you don't know. Perhaps you need a job, want advice from a perfect stranger, or need an acquaintance to help you get to know a new town. Regardless of your subject, a little creativity goes a long way when dealing with someone who has little to no personal investment in your life. Claire wanted a job on a television show, and so she wrote this letter to a contact she barely knew:

Hi James,

This is Claire Baker. You may recall that we were BFFs while working on the first season of The Office, *and I was hoping you might let me come by the set of your new show when you start shooting so I can see how it works. That way I can remind you of how awesome I am, and then hopefully your show will get picked up by the network for a full season and you can give me a job. Regardless, it'd be nice to see you again.*

Happy Martin Luther King Jr. Day!

Claire

Does this letter sound a little bizarre? Yes, but it worked because Claire knew her audience. She crafted a short, concise message with a little ridiculous banter to a comedy writer to demonstrate her sense of humor. She made her request immediately, kept the niceties for the end of the message, and stopped when she didn't need to say anything else. You don't need anything else when you ask a favor. If you can nail down those key items, you won't feel awkward and will improve your chances of getting what you want.

RUINING SOMEONE'S DAY WITH BAD NEWS

Nobody wants the role of the messenger, because the messenger gets shot. Whether you just came down with herpes, you have to tell a friend that their embarrassing Facebook photo became a meme, or you accidentally knocked your great aunt's ashes onto the carpet, it sucks to break bad news. While always awkward, you just have to find the right words and rip the Band-Aid off before you make matters worse.

Ashleigh married Roland and all was well. They had their fights like most married couples but nothing out of the ordinary. One day, Roland planned an exciting weekend. They went to Disneyland, decorated Christmas trees, and when all the fun came to a close, he handed her divorce papers. Roland wanted to give Ashleigh the element of surprise. As a result, he succeeded in breaking bad news in the worst way possible.

RIP OFF THE BAND-AID GENTLY

When breaking bad news, get to the point as soon as you can. When you waffle around the subject, you give the listener an opportunity to imagine the worst-case scenario. For example, imagine you just found out you have herpes and need to tell your partner.

BAD: *Hey, I need to talk to you about something. I'm not really sure how to put this. I noticed something weird about my body recently and went to the doctor. He ran an STD test, and, um, well, the results weren't great. It came back positive. So you might have herpes.*

GOOD: *I have some bad news. I just found out I have herpes. I haven't slept with anyone else since I met you, so maybe I contracted it in a previous relationship. Either way, you should get tested as soon as possible. I'm really sorry I put you in this position.*

In the bad version, you don't tell your partner what's wrong until the very end. Chances are he won't assume you have herpes, but rather something very serious like HIV. Additionally, you don't mention that you didn't cheat on your partner. If you were in his shoes, you'd want as much reassurance as possible upon hearing this kind of bad news. In the good version, you care more about your partner and look out for his health. You also get to the bad news immediately to avoid any speculation. While nobody wants to hear he might have herpes, you can soften the blow by empathizing and getting to the point.

REMINDING A FRIEND TO PAY UP OR DIE

Spencer was a scrawny intellectual who developed an obsession with sensual nightclub dancing later in life. He often spent up to eight hours in a sea of sweaty twenty-somethings, six nights a week. He funneled his small amount of disposable income into his hobby, living paycheck-to-paycheck and dance-to-dance. One summer, he and Claire received an invitation to their friend Ashleigh's second destination wedding and decided to travel together so they could split gas and lodging costs. Spencer's overactive bladder led to his absence whenever it came time to pay, so Claire ended up covering the majority of their expenses. Claire reminded him several times but never outright asked for the money. After a year of watching Spencer dance his money away, she just gave up. When you want a friend to pay you back, you often need to make an explicit request.

MAKE AN EXPLICIT REQUEST

When an unreliable friend asks to borrow money, or you can't afford the loan, just say no. While this might seem harsh, you don't want to have repeated awkward conversations about getting your money back.

Unfortunately, not all loans between friends happen by request. In Claire's situation, Spencer owed her money because she happened to pay and assumed he'd pay her back soon after. When you find yourself in this situation, you have a few ways to get your money back. First, you can ask your friend to pick up the next check (or few checks) when you go out to eat. If that doesn't do the trick, an explicit request often will. Here's an example:

> Hey Spencer, remember how you owe me $100 from Ashleigh's wedding? I was wondering if you could pay me back. I'm kind of tight on cash this month. Can you pay me back by the end of the week?

In this example, Claire not only asks Spencer for the money explicitly but also suggests a deadline. Additionally, by telling Spencer she's tight on cash this month Claire offers a problem that Spencer can solve.

It took Claire two years to realize she just had to ask for the money back, but making a request a week or two later can save you a lot of time, frustration, and lost money.

(LITERALLY) TAKE YOUR FRIEND TO THE BANK

Some friends require more effort than others when you try to get your money back. They may not have the money they owe you or just handle their finances irresponsibly. When a simple request fails, you need to push the issue.

Find out why they won't pay you back and make it clear that you need the money to live. If necessary, work out a payment plan so you know they will eventually repay what they owe. Most online banking sites offer bill pay services, and your friend can set theirs up so you receive a check from them on a regular basis. This way they don't have to remember to do anything.

A good friend will want to pay you back, even if it takes a little time and effort on your part to make it happen. However, sometimes friendships and relationships don't last as long as the debt. In these cases, you want to get your money back as quickly as possible. Online payment services like Pay-Pal, Amazon, and Square can help because they not only provide quick transactions but also allow your former friend to pay with a credit card. While you'll lose a little money due to service fees, at least you'll get the majority of your debt repaid. Offer to help your friend set up his account so you can ensure he actually does it.

Money between friends often leads to awkward situations, but if you approach the problem early and explicitly you can avoid these kinds of problems.

CONFRONTING
A CRAPPY FRIEND

Some people cope with the bad parts of life through laughter, the comfort of friends, and practiced optimism. Others drown themselves in debauchery. When friends engage in self-destructive behavior, they tend to share their misery with others. Sometimes you have to step in and call them out on their bullshit.

Helen spent years avoiding her vagina. She never truly understood the joy it could bring until her mid-twenties when she met a hyper-masculine fellow at a club and decided to find out. He brought her back to a bathroom stall, shoved her against a door, and ravaged her. While many women—and men, for that matter—might find getting plowed in a public toilet somewhat unappealing, Helen felt beautiful. She enjoyed this visceral brand of sex so much that it consumed her life.

Helen went home with strange men most nights and neglected everything else in her life. She came to work late and rarely saw her friends. She spent so much time seeking out men online and in clubs that she rarely saw anyone she actually knew. While at first she apologized, she quickly started to resent anyone who questioned her newfound sexual liberation. Helen treated her friends poorly and refused to talk to anyone who didn't support the needs of her vagina. At least, until Helen came down with a case of syphilis.

Unable to meet a new man—at least for a few weeks—she suddenly had time to spend with others. Her friends, however, had not forgiven her for her neglect. They left her to suffer with the affliction she had brought upon herself.

KNOW WHERE YOU STAND

When your friends engage in self-destructive behavior, you can't change them. You can only share your opinion and hope they change for the better. Once you understand that, you can figure out where you stand in the friendship and what you want to risk.

Most friends, no matter how lost, will listen to you if you voice your concern out of worry. They probably won't change based on what you say alone, but speaking your mind gives you the opportunity to let them know you'll listen if they want to talk. Also, if others have voiced concerns as well, your friend may start to pay attention to the message.

If not, you have to decide what you will sacrifice. You can beg and plead all you want, but in many cases you'll need to decide whether or not you want to put your friendship on the line. Figure out what's worse: dealing with your self-destructive friend who treats you poorly or making his recovery a condition of your friendship. Nobody likes to lose someone close, but you might have to acknowledge that he's already lost and risk making it official.

GIVE A KIND ULTIMATUM

If you reach the conclusion that you need to put your friendship on the line, do so kindly. Don't tell them off and cut them out of your life, but calmly explain why you can't spend time with them due to their current behavior. Let your friend know that they can call you to talk if they need help and want to change, but otherwise you will not see or speak to them. Do not allow room for debate. Do not entertain any insults. Say what you need to say and move on. If they want help and want to change, everybody wins. If not, you have to let them go. You can't change someone who doesn't want to change, and at least one of you will feel better once the hurt fades away.

DEALING WITH A DEADBEAT ROOMMATE

Sometimes you move in with a best friend. Other times you go to Craigslist and end up renting a room from a sixty-five-year-old woman and her six very fragrant cats. When you need a place to live, you can't always pick and choose from the best roommates. But when you sign a lease with a turd of a landlord, you'll need to find a way out.

Claire needed a roommate quickly and rushed into a lease with Chlora Schlotsky, a nymphomaniac in a constant state of heart failure. Chlora brought home a variety of men for vigorous intercourse while she remained connected to a small heart regulator next to her bed. Perhaps due to a combination of her charm and pity for her condition, she managed to acquire a large rotation of casual sex partners. They came in the late evening and early morning with greater regularity than her dysfunctional heartbeat. With rattling beds at all hours, Claire found little opportunity to sleep. Furthermore, sex made Chlora ravenous. Many nights, Chlora would find her way into the refrigerator and eat through Claire's stash of cheese. Combined with alcohol, this often led to violent vomiting. Sometimes Chlora made it to the toilet, other times she just made it to the couch. When you sign a lease with another person, you can't always know what problems he'll bring. You may not succeed in getting rid of a terrible roommate like Chlora, but you can try.

DISCUSS THE PROBLEM

Whether your roommate is too loud, leaves bodily fluids around the house, loves heroin, doesn't pay rent on time (or at all), or you just can't stand each other, you'll need to first discuss the problem so you can find any possible solution. People like Chlora, who have loud sex, sometimes don't realize what kind of impact they have until the drywall starts to crack or someone actually tells them. You may have a crazy roommate, however, and get absolutely nowhere with a conversation. Regardless of the outcome, you need to start talking, otherwise you won't know whether to take extreme measures or not.

REVIEW YOUR LEASE

Most leases make both roommates liable for the entirety of the rent, but some don't. You should review your lease because you may have the right to move out if you find a suitable replacement—one who doesn't mind the sounds of a wall-pounding orgasm instead of an alarm, of course.

When scanning through your lease, look for the terms *jointly* and/or *severally liable. Jointly liable* means you and your roommate bear the responsibility to pay the full rent even if one of you comes up short. For example, if Chlora missed a payment due to eternal penetration, Claire would get screwed in the process. *Severally liable*, on the other hand, means you only have to pay your portion of the rent. If your roommate doesn't pay, she'll get in trouble and you won't. Some leases include both terms—joint and several *liability*—which still require you to pay the full rent if your roommate does not but allows you to sue said roommate for her delinquent amount.

For the most part, these terms only help resolve monetary disputes. That said, you may have an easier time leaving before your lease ends if you are severally liable.

TALK TO YOUR LANDLORD

If you can't stand your roommate and want out, you can talk to your landlord about finding a replacement for yourself. Explain your situation and your landlord may let you out of the lease if you can obtain another co-tenant that meets his standards. Sometimes you can't get into the details. You wouldn't tell a landlord you want out because your roommate won't stop having sex, eating cheese, and vomiting all over the couch. When your circumstances are more delicate, just say you can't get along and need to go. Several liability will make it easier to negotiate this because you and your roommate have, for all intents and purposes, separate contracts. Joint liability, on the other hand, means your landlord must draft a new lease to replace you—something he or she probably won't want to do. Nevertheless, a kind landlord may help and you won't know unless you ask.

PLAN AHEAD

While you may not get out of your lease, before you try you need to have a plan for where you'll live next. You don't want to end up with another shitty roommate, so start looking for a new one in advance. Before you sign a new lease with another human being, set ground rules. Talk about potentially awkward subjects in advance so they don't turn into huge dilemmas like Claire and Chlora's. Not only will this help you avoid future problems, but you'll get to know your new roommate a little better before you move in together and—hopefully—find a friend instead of an enemy.

RECOVERING FROM AUTOCORRECT MISTAKES

Cell phones and computers have changed the way we communicate with people. We send emails and text messages while traveling, getting drunk, and taking a dump. At times it increases our efficiency, at others it muddles the lines of communication. Be smart about how you use your device.

Stefan was a big blonde tennis coach who only slept with women in China. He taught several clients privately, and when they were good enough, invited them to join his group clinics. This was his intention with Dante, a shy but passionate new customer. Stefan meant to say, "I want you to come to class," but, because of a few typos, it autocorrected to "I want to come in your ass." Stefan only realized his mistake when he saw Dante's response: "Wow, really? How did you know?" After considering changing his sexual orientation in order to cover up his mistake, he had to come clean with Dante. Avoid putting your genitals in awkward situations by paying closer attention to your phone's decisions.

AVOID THE MISTAKE

The first step is prevention. If your phone keeps changing "I think I got what I needed" to "I hobo I dog what I beeded," it's time to turn off autocorrect. If you use an iPhone, you can disable it by going to the keyboard section of your "general" settings. You can also temporarily disable the feature by typing everything before the letter *z*. Once you've typed a *z*, touch and drag the cursor to place it immediately before it, and none of what you type will be affected. This is especially handy when you're trying to type in another language. Android and other phones vary, but going into "language and keyboard" in the settings will usually give you the option to disable autocorrect or autocomplete.

TAKE A FEW SECONDS

Sometimes you'll immediately notice that you told your friend about some delicious poop instead of food. Or that the person you texted about a hot date is actually your mom. Using a text message app like Cancel SMS or Undo SMS will give you a couple minutes to cancel your message once you've sent it. If you use Gmail, you can set up a feature that handles the same thing. Under settings, go to labs and enable Undo Send. This will give you about twenty seconds to cancel the message. The easiest way to notice an error, however, is to look at your device while you're writing a message. If you commonly have embarrassing autocorrect issues, spend less time multitasking and make sure you're happy with the text before you hit send.

REPAIR THE DAMAGE

Sometimes it's more than just a simple typo, like when Stefan inadvertently offered to put his dick in Dante's anus. The best way to handle such a situation is to apologize and laugh it off. You might want to give the person a call after it happens to avoid additional autocorrect confusion. Stefan was dreading his next lesson with Dante, but once they were able to joke about it in person, the tension was lifted and it became a funny moment to look back on. These days, people often send messages while driving, exercising, or having sex. Your friends and acquaintances will likely blame your technology for the error instead of your distraction.

We rely on our devices to fix our mistakes, but they often end up doing more harm than good. Paying attention to what you write, double-checking messages before you send them, and turning off autocorrect can help. But when everything fails, you might as well throw up your hands and enjoy the fact that your phone tried to decide where you would ejaculate.

SAVING FACE AFTER AN ACCIDENTAL INSULT

Insulting people can be great, especially when they deserve it. But sometimes things come out accidentally and you wish you'd never said anything. Learn to remove your foot from your mouth as painlessly as possible.

Trey was a professor who loved to teach through origami. Nathan met him at a museum exhibit where they bonded over their mutual love of Japanese culture. A few days later, Trey picked Nathan up at his house so they could attend a Yo-Yo Ma concert. As soon as Trey started driving, Nathan began to fear for his life. Though they had over an hour to get to the venue, Trey kept speeding, cutting everyone off, and nearly crashing the car. To distract himself from the oncoming nausea, Nathan texted his friend Ben to complain about the situation. Moments later Trey's phone emitted a buzzing sound. Nathan realized he had sent, "I'm with an asshole who drives like a maniac and I think he's going to kill us" to Trey. Nathan tried to delete the message off Trey's phone, but Trey got to it faster, almost hitting a bus in the process. Nathan used this as an opportunity to discuss Trey's driving habits, but would have preferred to bring it up more diplomatically.

INSULT PEOPLE TO THEIR FACE

This may seem like strange advice, but think of it this way: it's better to apologize for insulting someone than to apologize because he found out you insulted him. If someone you don't know very well does something that bothers you, you'll probably tell your friends or family about the situation instead of confronting him. This causes two problems: a) the issue doesn't get resolved, and b) if you complain to enough people, the comments will probably get back to the person. Worry less about offending someone and more about communicating directly and honestly.

Of course, you don't want to walk around telling everyone you think he is ugly or stupid. However, there are circumstances where you'll eventually have to share your true feelings. For example, if you can't stand someone and he keeps trying to be your friend, you need to be forthright. He will probably be insulted, but less so than if he heard about it through gossip.

In Nathan's case, he was scared for his safety and perturbed by the way Trey handled a car. Had he spent a minute or two thinking about how to express that instead of texting Ben, he could have solved the problem without coming off like an asshole.

DON'T MAKE UP AN EXCUSE

Once you've accidentally insulted someone, don't try to backtrack. Nathan first tried to make up reasons why Trey shouldn't look at his phone while he attempted to delete the message. Once he saw it, Nathan tried to pretend it was a joke, but he quickly had to tell Trey exactly what had happened. Trey was initially a little hurt, but by the end of the night they could both laugh about the faux pas. A candid conversation leads to forgiveness much faster than a bunch of BS.

You might insult someone without even knowing it. A benign comment sometimes comes off as mean because of a sensitivity you didn't know about. For instance, making a dumb joke about your friend getting fat while he inhales an ice cream sundae might hit a nerve if he was once a chubby kid who got bullied. Don't try to take back the comment or come up with a fake justification for the joke. Explain that you didn't know about his past issue and you didn't realize it would hurt him. If he's a friend, he should be able to tell that you are being sincere.

APOLOGIZE IF YOU CARE; MOVE ON IF YOU DON'T

When we accidentally insult someone we don't like, we often feel guilty. The guilt comes from the fact that we said something mean we didn't necessarily plan on sharing. Our response is usually to apologize or try to repair the relationship in some way. However, that may not be necessary. If you don't like someone, don't waste your time making things better. Use your mistake to get rid of someone you never wanted in your life.

If you do like the person, he probably cares about you in some way. A genuine apology should suffice to repair the friendship and move on. Don't overthink what you're going to say or how you're going to say it, just be frank about what happened.

If the victim is your boss or your in-laws, you'll probably need to apologize to maintain a healthy relationship. However, it can be an opportunity to politely talk about whatever issue you're having. Think about how you would feel if the tables were turned and speak to them in the way you would want to be addressed.

COMING OUT OF
THE BIG GAY CLOSET

Back in the day you couldn't come out of the closet without risking your well-being. Nowadays many young people can embrace their big gay dreams without too much trouble. That said, bigotry still exists in changing times, and, even when it doesn't, you'll find some of the most awkward attempts at acceptance.

Nathan came out to his parents at age fifteen. They supported him and wanted to do everything they could to help. Parents know a little bit about their job when they first get into it, but few receive an education on what to do when they find out their son enjoys the company of men. After Nathan first came out, his parents turned to the professionals they found on the Internet and scheduled a big gay surprise weekend to celebrate the occasion and signal their acceptance.

Bright and early Saturday morning, Mom and Dad woke Nathan up to take him to a PFLAG* meeting. Upon arrival they discovered the topic: transgender teens. Later, they took him to a gay youth center to meet other kids like him. They neglected to notice that the youth center was actually a homeless shelter until they picked him up several hours later. Finally, his parents took him out to dinner at one of the few gay-friendly restaurants in their town. While in the bathroom, an older man propositioned him in the handicapped stall. Despite their best efforts, even the most accepting parents make a lot of mistakes when they learn that they have a gay child. When

*For the uninitiated, that's Parents and Friends of Lesbians and Gays.

you come out, remember that even the best people need time to adjust.

After giving his parents time to adjust, Nathan came out at his school. Rather than telling a few people and letting the information spread, he got up on stage at an assembly and blurted it out. Some kids applauded his bravery, but he lost most of his friends and received a death threat from one. Whatever cards you draw in the coming out process, you always end up with a mixed bag. Some people will love you. Others will hate you. Nathan made it through the rough patches by concentrating on the good.

CREATE YOUR OWN SUPPORT GROUP

Coming out creates a lot of stress and you need to know that you have a few people (or more) to lean on when times get tough. If you get a few negative responses—even from strangers—it can feel like the whole world hates you for something you can't control. You need to focus on the good, and you can't without positive forces in your life.

Before you come out to your parents and friends, make sure you have a support system. If absolutely nobody knows, let the Internet help you. Find online support groups with other people who can empathize and share their experiences. (Note: don't meet anyone from these groups in person or provide any personal information during this process.) Next, figure out a good order of divulgence. Come out to the people most likely to accept you first and work your way up to the more difficult ones. Not only will this ease you into the process and build confidence, but you'll also grow your support system as you go along.

DON'T EXPLODE INTO YOUR SEXUALITY

Share the news of your sexuality gently. Don't force it on anyone. While you have every right to express yourself, if you make the news a big deal it can become a big deal. Like most people, your sexuality only represents a part of you. When you come out, you want people to realize that you're sharing a piece of yourself, and not your only characteristic.

The same advice applies to your personal behavior. Once your sexuality becomes a matter of public knowledge and not a secret tucked into a dark corner of the closet, you'll want to embrace it. Suddenly you get to be a gay man or woman in public, visit gay establishments, and have access to a lot of sex you didn't before. Don't act like a necrophiliac at a funeral home. You have time to explore your sexuality and experience the new freedoms that coming out affords. Too much of a good thing quickly becomes a bad thing, so take it slow.

DON'T COME OUT TO ANYONE YOU (LITERALLY) CAN'T AFFORD TO LOSE

You should come out to everyone eventually, but sometimes you need to wait. When someone who supports you financially may not support your sexuality, you may want to hold off on the truth.

Most gay youth only find themselves in this situation with excessively conservative parents when they either live at home or rely on their parents for assistance while they try to make their own way. You don't want to come out to your mom or dad if they provide you with something you need. If you have legitimate fears of an altercation, wait until you no longer need their financial support. Come out to them when they have nothing to hold over you but their affection. That puts you on equal ground because you can do the same to them. Make your presence in their life require their acceptance. While an antigay parent may not welcome you with open arms simply because they miss you, with enough patience you can get them to listen and start a conversation. The impossible can happen. Many ultraconservative parents accept their queer kids over time. You just have to stay patient, ignore their ridiculous behavior, and work with them toward loving you for who you are.

VISITING SICK PEOPLE IN THE HOSPITAL

Going to see a friend who injured herself during a challenging lacrosse match isn't a big deal. Going to see someone sick with cancer or AIDS really sucks. You have to deal with repeated visits to a place that smells bad and has gross people everywhere. Plus, you have to pretend that your friend or relative looks healthy when his face reminds you of the sky on an overcast day. Remember that things will always be worse for him than they are for you, because you get to live and he has to suffer and die.

Jasmine was a highly emotional Greek Orthodox woman who obsessed over looking thin. She was devastated when the doctors diagnosed her cousin Adelpha with cancer. Jasmine sought out the best care and prayed for her every day. She even stopped asking the Lord to help her lose weight so he could focus all his efforts on Adelpha. Jasmine's daughter Tessa accompanied her to the hospital the first time they went. While everyone fawned over Adelpha and told her how great she looked, Jasmine burst into tears. She acted more upset than her cousin's husband and daughter and her sobs began to upset them. It was very difficult to lie to Adelpha about her imminent death when Jasmine kept complaining about how much she'd miss her when she was gone.

Eventually Adelpha's daughter called Tessa to tell her she couldn't let her mom come to the hospital anymore. Her daily crying fits upset everyone and they couldn't handle it. Jasmine was so angry that she didn't eat for five days, at least gaining the satisfaction of losing another pound. It's okay to be sad when someone close to you is going to die, but don't be selfish and make it all about you.

PUT YOURSELF IN THEIR HOSPITAL GOWN

It can be hard to know how to talk to sick or injured people. They have tubes coming out of them, they don't have much energy, and they may even seem like a different person. Instead of trying to figure out the nicest thing to say, think about how you'd like that person to talk to you if you switched places. You probably wouldn't want to talk about your condition at all and would prefer whatever normal communication you usually have. While there's nothing wrong with being encouraging about someone's recovery, try not to focus on that. You don't have to avoid the subject entirely, as you don't want to make it seem like he can't talk about it if he wants to. But the person you're visiting would probably prefer for you to share some stories instead of discussing the mechanics of his catheter.

Your goal in visiting is to brighten their day and distract them from their hardship. If you go to see older relatives with whom you don't have that much to talk about, you can bring pictures to show them or an activity like a deck of cards. If the patient is younger, bring a new video game or some movies to watch. Don't worry too much about how to talk about illness and just try to be positive and entertaining. If he doesn't want to see you or have any visitors at all, respect his wishes. You might also feel a little uncomfortable having your colleagues visit you when you're pooping in a bag.

USE THE RING THEORY

Sometimes the sick person is close to you, like in Jasmine's case. However, Adelpha's disease affected Adelpha, her daughter, and her husband more than it affected Jasmine. It was okay for Jasmine to be sad, but it wasn't okay for her to yell at them when they banned her from the hospital. Psychologist Susan Silk recommends using the Ring Theory to determine whom it's okay to complain to.

Write down the sick person's name and draw a circle around it. Then write down the name of the person most affected by his illness and draw a circle around the name. This could be his parents, boyfriend, or child. Continue to draw rings for each concerned individual. A close friend would go in a small ring, a boss or colleague in a larger one. Wherever you are in the hierarchy, just make sure you don't complain to anyone in a smaller circle than yourself. Bitching goes outward and support goes inward. It's normal for you to be sad if your best friend is battling cancer, but it's not okay to complain about how much it's disturbing your social life to her parents. Use the people in bigger circles for that; they'll understand what you're going through without feeling offended.*

Being the next of kin can be a huge challenge. Besides the emotional difficulties, you'll probably have to take time off work, help make medical decisions, and put everything in your life on hold for your loved one. Turn to the people in the outer circles to help with some of the smaller tasks so you can spend more time with the person who matters. Even if they can't make the sick person get better, helping you will make them feel needed and give them a chance to do their part.

GET EMOTIONAL SUPPORT FROM SOMEONE WHO HAS DISTANCE

Even if the sick person is your best friend, you have no idea what the other people in his life are going through. It may seem natural to speak to his girlfriend about how devastated you are that he's paralyzed, but it may also come off as selfish to someone who is in a sensitive place. His girlfriend will be the one dealing with the paralysis on a daily basis and she probably has no idea how she's going to handle it. Offer her help and make it clear that you're there for whatever she needs, but get your comfort from someone who's not involved. Talk to one of your friends who has the emotional space to be there for you because he doesn't need to be there for the injured party. Just like it's your job to be there for your best friend and his girlfriend, it's the job of the people close to you to make sure you're okay. Jasmine thought she could cry and moan in despair in front of Adelpha's children because they were going through the same thing, but she was just making it more difficult for them. Jasmine's husband was the person she should have been getting emotional support from.

Watching a friend or relative suffer through an illness can be very challenging, but it's important to remember that he is the one suffering through it. During this time, it's all about him, and any help or support you need should be provided by the people in your life who are less directly affected by the situation.

---

* Susan Silk & Barry Goldman, "How not to say the wrong thing," LA Times, April 7, 2013, http://articles.latimes.com/2013/apr/07/opinion/la-oe-0407-silk-ring-theory-20130407.

GIVING CONDOLENCES (THAT DON'T SUCK)

Unless you enjoy serial murder, you probably don't enjoy death. Nobody likes to confront mortality and few people handle it well. Nevertheless, giving your condolences feels a lot harder than it should be, because we've all dealt with loss in some form. You just have to find a way to relate.

Lola was a bitch—not only because she was a female dog but because she incited hate and loathing in everyone she met. She bit, she barked, she took large dumps all over the house after swallowing huge portions of human food that her stomach couldn't digest. Lola was hard to love up until the day she succumbed to her own desires. During a dinner party, a guest brought a pot brownie as a gift. Lola found and consumed it, came down with the munchies, and chewed her way through a briefcase in order to eat a roll of cash totaling $2,000. Upon her death, guests found it difficult to console the family because they had nothing nice to say. We can't always understand why our friends love certain pets, or even people, but when they die it helps to show a little sympathy. Although death brings a lot of discomfort to conversation, if you take the right approach you can feel good about what you said instead of awkward.

KNOW THE DETAILS

Before you give your condolences, you want to know what happened to the deceased. You don't want to ask someone in mourning something along the lines of, "So did she die of anal cancer?" Most people prefer not to discuss the details, so get them from someone less affected by the death. This person may also know who is doing what to help the family and the specifics of the funeral arrangements so you don't have to bother the bereaved.

FIND A WAY TO RELATE

In your life you've dealt with loss, if not death specifically. Whether a journal with all your secrets or a significant other you loved, when something important suddenly disappears you can feel like a part of you went missing as well. While you never want to compare a lesser loss to the death of a loved one, you can use this sentiment to understand how a friend or family member feels. On the outside, they seem like a complete mess with little control over their emotions. We all lose ourselves sometimes, so before giving your condolences it helps to recall when you felt similarly.

In many situations, you don't need to say much. Let the bereaved know that you're sorry to hear about their loss, but ask them how they're doing. Obviously death sucks, and they won't tell you all about the joys of life, but this offers them an opportunity to share their feelings and talk with you if they want to. As silly as it may seem, asking this question can make a big difference because it starts a conversation and doesn't feel like a generic statement by the time you both finish talking. This conversation may last a while, so set aside at least an hour to talk in case you need it.

You don't have to say anything kind about the dead. In fact, you don't have to say anything at all. When Lola the dog died from eating a wad of cash, people tried to find relevant ways to compliment her and pretend she wasn't terrible. "She was . . . loved" and "She was a good eater" didn't make much of a difference to the family. When you allow for a conversation, however, the bereaved can tell you about the things that mattered to them and you can simply agree. That way you don't have to come up with any false statements or think of the perfect thing to say.

OFFER TO HELP IN SPECIFIC, CONCRETE WAYS

If you feel inclined to help the close friends and family the deceased left behind, offer it in specific ways.

DON'T DO THIS: *Let me know if there's anything I can do to help.*
DO THIS: *Let me know if I can babysit the kids, drive you anywhere, or make you dinner.*

A vague offer to help puts the burden on the bereaved and makes them reach out to you if they want anything. Often times, when dealing with a loss, you have no motivation to do the little things in life like make food or pay the bills. You also feel completely ridiculous asking someone else to do this for you. If you really want to help, offer specific things. For example, many people make or bring food. If you feel close enough, you can offer to make a meal with sentimental value. For example, if a husband loses his wife and has to take care of his children, you could offer to make the kids' favorite meal. Death often feels sudden, and happy memories—food-related or otherwise—can help ease the bereaved through the transition. Everyone deals with death a little bit differently, however, so always offer before you take action.

PART IV

DATING

Now and again, some couples get lucky. They meet as friends, find out they really like spending time with each other, secretly harbor a physical attraction, and finally decide to make that attraction known. If only all relationships progressed so naturally, we'd have more successful romances. Most of us, however, get to go on awkward dates and make embarrassing mistakes.

Blind dates hurt the most. You go out with someone you've probably never seen before—at least not in real life—and only know a little bit about. You talk about your interests, your hopes and dreams, and can feel like you just had a decent job interview if you only manage to skirt by. Sure, you can take risks, but you might end up sharing your favorite dead-baby joke only to find out your date's would-be sister was thrown away in a trash can. When you put your best foot forward with someone you barely know, you'll probably kick him or her with it a few times. You can't absolve yourself of that risk, but you can learn to approach dating without frequent disaster.

Dates can go well and blossom into relationships or they can die an awkward death. When things go poorly, most people resort to ignoring texts and calls until the other person seemingly takes the hint, but that leaves them without closure and prolongs discomfort. If they go well for a while but eventually die out, you get to experience the joys of a break-up conversation. Of course, some relationships work out for the best but they have their awkward moments as well. For example, if you don't fall in love at the exact same time you can cause a rift by disclosing too soon or too late.

Relationships take work, and you can't escape awkwardness, but you can learn to handle it well. If you muster up a little courage, you can approach the scariest parts in a relationship without getting too uncomfortable. After all, what is a little awkwardness when you might find love?

GOING ON A FIRST DATE THAT DOESN'T SUCK

First dates can be scary, confusing, or—worst of all—boring. By preparing a little you can have an evening that's more fun than awkward.

Ben set up Tessa with his friend Justin. She had been feeling under the weather after a difficult course of antibiotics, and Ben thought it would be good for her to go out. Justin asked her how she was doing, so she was honest and said she wasn't great. When she mentioned that she had an infection, Justin asked if it was an STD. She tried to reassure him by explaining that she just had a vaginal and anal yeast infection. Once they got a drink, Justin asked her to tell him about something in which she was interested. She enthusiastically described her passion for learning about conjoined twins. She was fascinated with the idea that each used one arm and one leg and wondered if they traditionally shared an iPhone. Justin found her strange nature endearing and got to know Tessa well enough to find out she wasn't insane. Tessa didn't necessarily have the best approach, but she created an evening that was out of the ordinary.

BE INTERESTING

There's a lot of pressure on a first date, especially if you've never met the person. While you don't want to be too forward, you also don't want to be boring. It's more important to be charming and funny than to be polite.

While Tessa's conjoined-twin description was unusual, it showed Justin how unique she was and provided a good conversation starter. While you probably don't want to dispense as much information as Tessa did, sharing specific things about yourself will help the relationship progress. Figuring out what to say on a date isn't always easy, so think about how you act in other circumstances. What are some stories that have made your friends laugh? Toward the end of the evening, Tessa told Justin about the time she got stuck in a strip club in Tijuana. It was a good way for her to gauge Justin's sense of humor, and it inspired him to tell her about some of his unusual travel stories. If you're not a natural conversationalist, practice telling the stories to other people before you try them on a date.

ASK THE RIGHT QUESTIONS

The best dates involve mutual story sharing and discussion of common interests. However, you'll probably have to ask some questions along the way to keep the conversation going and get to know your date better. Asking questions shows your date you're interested and gives a chance to share some personal stuff too. Make sure you don't just pick a generic topic—ask something that will generate an interesting answer. You want your questions to facilitate the conversation, not seem like an interrogation. Ask things that you would want to be asked and that you would feel comfortable answering, and your date will probably ask some of the same ones in return. Here are some examples of bad questions:

BAD
- *What's one of your favorite quotes?*
- *What's your "why" in life?*
- *How was your day?*
- *What's your favorite body part?*

While some of these questions might be fine in other circumstances, they're not ideal on a first date because they won't help lead to an interesting conversation. Someone you just met will probably answer "how was your day" with a simple answer like "fine." Even if they feel comfortable picking their favorite body part, it will probably also be a one-word response. Here are some examples of good questions:

GOOD

- *What are some of the TV shows you watch?*
- *What was the last good book you read?*
- *Where have you traveled to so far? What's a place you've never been that you really want to visit?*

All of these questions are relatively easy to answer, as opposed to coming up with a quote on the spot. Furthermore, they'll help you identify common interests. If you date doesn't watch TV or movies and you live for entertainment, you'll quickly become aware of a potential problem. However, it's likely that he's read at least one good book in his life and taken at least one trip. Even if you don't have any common ground with these answers, you might get a reading recommendation or a good story about his first excursion abroad.

PICK AN ACTIVITY

It's great when you can spend hours at a coffee shop talking to someone, but that doesn't always happen right away. If you're shy or worried about filling an evening, plan something fun to do. Presumably you spent a little time getting to know your date before you asked him out. Think of his interests and suggest a related activity. If you both like art, pick a museum where you can spend the afternoon. If nothing else, the exhibit you see together will give you something to discuss. Low-key physical activities like bowling or mini golf can also be good for breaking the ice. Run it by your date first—planning what you'll do and where you'll go is part of the getting-to-know-you process. Whatever you choose, you'll get points for being creative and thinking about what the person would actually enjoy.

You only get one first date, so make it memorable. You don't have to rent a horse and carriage to impress your date. Pick something fun to do, show an interest in the person you're with, and share some funny stories. If you're nervous, remember that he agreed to go on the date. There's a good chance he already likes you, and all you have to do is remind him why.

TELLING SOMEONE YOU LIKE HIM

You can compliment a nice shirt. When faced with complimenting a personality, however, you start to feel vulnerable because clothing can't reject you but a human can. Nevertheless, if you don't tell someone you like him you end up rejecting yourself.

Talia harbored feelings for Ben throughout college. She adjusted her class schedule to coincide with his as often as possible, offered to help him whenever he needed it, and tried her best to spend any kind of time with him. Ben, however, didn't have the slightest clue of how she felt. While a more adept man might have picked up on the hints, Talia never made a clear attempt. Early on she asked to join him for lunch. In a more bold attempt, she asked him to come home and help her with her laundry—which he didn't understand meant sex. Knowing Ben enjoyed bathroom humor, Talia bought him a piece of fossilized dinosaur poop for his birthday—which he accepted uncomfortably. While she never had a bad intention, Talia didn't take a chance with her feelings. She instead tried sending veiled messages, hoping that Ben would ask her out. If Ben rejected her it would hurt, but never as much as four years of feeling ignored and unwanted.

DON'T PLAN

While planning can get you a lot of places, you don't have to bother when you want to tell someone how you feel because you only have to make a short statement. When you plan, you convince yourself that you're about to undertake this incredibly large and scary task. You figuratively climb a mountain to proclaim your feelings rather than just saying them. If you spend time doing anything in advance, assure yourself how little this one life event actually matters and what kind of damage you can do by waiting.

When you tell someone you like him, you might get a disappointing response. You'll feel somewhat bad but you get the gift of moving on. When you plan ahead before you tell him, you actually lose something significant if that person doesn't return your feelings. The more time you invest, the more important the proclamation becomes. A negative response means you lose all that time you spent trying to figure out how to get a yes. In the end, all the little things you do to woo a romantic partner pale in comparison to who you actually are.

Spend a little time getting to know people, and if you realize you like one of them just let him know. You don't have to put any pressure on him or yourself. If you take a lighthearted approach and don't add unnecessary weight to the moment, a negative answer won't stop you from pursuing other options in the future. You might just get a positive one, too.

JUST DO IT

When you like someone, you really only have one course of action: tell him. You don't have to complicate matters. You just have to summon a little courage and say the following:

I like you. Would you like to go out sometime?

Although not an incredibly bold statement, we turn it into one by worrying how the other person will react and then convince ourselves we shouldn't say anything at all. You just have to say it and hope for the best. Rejection stings, but with enough of it you learn not to take it too personally. You can't be the right choice for everyone, so look at rejection as a puzzle piece that didn't quite fit. You don't give up on a puzzle because one piece didn't work out, nor do you sit around staring at it and wonder if it'll work. You have to try, fail, and try again. Rejection happens often, but not always. Take a risk, press on after a failure, and enjoy the rewards that will eventually come.

TELLING SOMEONE YOU DON'T LIKE THEM

The world contains republicans, democrats, hipsters, gun-rights crusaders, members of PETA, motorcyclists, reality TV stars, other drivers, writers, and many more distinct groups filled with opinionated people. Even if you manage to get along with a diverse crowd, you probably don't want to date them. That's okay, so long as you learn to break the news clearly and respectfully.

Jo-Beth fell in love with Ember the minute she laid eyes on her ironic cut-off jeans and ugly Christmas sweater. They both worked the inventory night shift at a local sock warehouse, cataloging the daily surplus of foot apparel. Jo-Beth loved to talk and Ember enjoyed listening, so the nights passed by quickly and both girls grew fond of each other. One night, while packing hosiery, Jo-Beth worked up the courage to ask Ember out on a date. Ember, however, wasn't romantically interested because Jo-Beth had an oily complexion and lived in a tent. Additionally, Ember wasn't a lesbian.

Nevertheless, Jo-Beth convinced her to go out just one time on a day cruise. Although Ember didn't like boats or sex with women, she found herself enjoying her time on the water. Jo-Beth figured that Ember's newfound appreciation of boats might have opened her up to other new possibilities and went in for a kiss. Ember didn't want to be rude, so she let the kiss happen but said no to Jo-Beth's offer to go out again. Jo-Beth continued her pursuit and Ember would politely deny each time, never getting to the root of the problem. Eventually, Ember quit her job at the sock warehouse to get away from Jo-Beth when she could have simply confronted the situation. When you need to tell someone you don't like her, romantically or otherwise, you have to say so in explicit terms.

BE HONEST, BUT DON'T BE A DICK

If you don't like someone romantically (or otherwise), you have to tell her clearly or she'll find any and all glimmers of hope in your wishy-washy wording. Although such statements may seem harsh at times, you can communicate clearly without turning into an asshole.

> **DO THIS:** *I'm not interested in you romantically.*
> **DON'T DO THIS:** *I don't think we should date* **OR** *I can't go out with you.*

When you say, "I don't think we can" or "I can't" you give a passive message with an unclear motivation. This leaves open the possibility that a fixable problem exists that your romantic suitor can solve. When you say you're not interested (romantically), however, you make your feelings clear. She can still ask why, but so long as you continue to make definitive statements she can't do much to change the reality you present. Of course, simply stating, "I don't want a relationship with you" or "I'm not interested in you romantically" comes off a little harsh. You can soften the blow with the tone of your voice and a little extra explanation:

> *I still like you, but I just don't want a romantic relationship with you.*

When you say this, you will hurt the former friend. You can't get around this uncomfortable reality. That said, the pain will heal faster if you don't leave any room for interpretation and let her know she needs to move on. If you lead her on, you'll only end up hurting her more in the end.

SAYING "I LOVE YOU" BY ACCIDENT

Everybody says, "I love you," but not everyone means it. Sometimes you're caught up in the moment and it just comes out of your mouth. If you don't want your relationship to suffer, come clean sooner rather than later.

Claire had feelings for her tennis partner, Zach. For months she tried to bring it up or figure out if he felt the same way, but something always interfered. Once she lifted her head up to serve, and a goose pooped in her mouth. She immediately vomited and had to go home to brush her teeth for several hours. Another time she hit herself in the head with her own racket and gave herself a concussion. By the time they finally managed to have dinner together, she'd spent so much time overthinking the situation that she blurted out, "I love you."

Claire was attracted to Zach and interested in the possibility of a relationship with him, but she didn't love him. She knew he had a good backhand, but she really didn't know him at all. Zach was confused about where this came from, and Claire was too embarrassed to explain how she actually felt. She changed the subject, and both of them pretended nothing had happened because they weren't sure what to do. What could have turned into a good relationship remained a slightly awkward sports partnership.

WHEN THE RESPONSE IS POSITIVE

If you are in a relationship, your boyfriend or girlfriend might be thrilled with your declaration. Whether or not she was planning on saying the same thing, she might at least be flattered that you feel that way. Bring up the faux pas as soon as you can. Tell her where you're at, and why you think you said, "I love you." Take this slightly unfortunate opportunity to share your actual feelings. It's possible that you will love this person, but you need more time with her before you get to that stage. It's also possible that you're in a dead-end relationship, and this would be a good time to end it. Figure out what you're truly feeling before you have this talk so you can have a clear, honest conversation. If you're worried about hurting the person by revealing the truth, don't. It'll be much worse if she finds out later that you didn't mean it. Make sure she knows how much you do care about her, and she'll understand that you didn't mean any harm.

WHEN THE RESPONSE IS NEGATIVE

Perhaps you don't love the person you're with yet, but you do care about him a lot. A bad reaction to your accidental revelation might scare you into thinking the relationship is going poorly. Instead of ignoring what happened and trying to figure out what the other person is thinking, say you want to schedule some time to talk. Ask for an opinion about what you said, be honest about why you think the words came out, tell how you really feel, and apologize if you made him uncomfortable. Doing these four things allows you to take responsibility for what happened, but also takes some of the pressure off you. Had Claire done this the next time she saw Zach, they could have cleared the air. Zach would have been relieved to hear that the situation was not as extreme as he thought and that Claire was simply nervous. Claire could have found out how Zach felt about her, and they could have decided whether or not to go on a date. Either way, it would have beat the awkwardness she left in place and given both of them the answers they were looking for.

Use this as a time for both of you to talk about the relationship and how things are going. If you want to move forward with the person, it's important for everyone to be on the same page. If neither of you wants to move forward with you, it's better to find out before you are in love for real.

Saying I love you when you don't mean it might feel like peeing your pants in public. But just like you can wash the pants, you can cleanly move on with your relationship.

RESPONDING TO "I LOVE YOU" WHEN YOU JUST ... DON'T

You know that feeling of always wanting to be with your significant other? You smile when you see him, enjoy his presence, miss him when he leaves, and know you can always count on him when times get tough? No, you don't, because you don't love your significant other. That's okay—at least, until he decides he's in love with you. If your partner shares his feelings, don't lie or panic. The right response can dismiss discomfort pretty easily.

Helen and John found each other through the wonder of the Internet and their shared love for BDSM—that's bondage, domination, sadism and masochism, for the uninitiated. Despite living on different ends of the country, they visited each other often to engage in elaborate sexual games with each other. One evening, Helen found herself hog-tied on the bed. John left her in this position to go run some errands. Normally he'd return in thirty minutes or an hour, but time slowly passed and Helen began to get irritated. Four hours later, John came back to find Helen still bound and filled with rage. A long, tiresome argument followed and, at the end, Helen admitted she loved John. Although John didn't love Helen, he lied, hoping to appease her, effusively asking her to move in with him.

Helen moved out to his side of the country, leaving her friends and family behind. After three months, John cheated on her and admitted he wasn't in love. While he didn't toss Helen out onto the streets, she spent an awkward month with him while she tried to find a new place to live in a city she barely knew.

STAY POSITIVE AND NEVER LIE

When you don't love someone, don't say that you do. Obvious in the light of day, sure, but not so much when you have to react in a split second. It helps to think about this scenario before it occurs so you know what you'll say if it does. If you love your partner, you have an easy answer. If not, you need to know how you'll tell him the truth. Most of the time, a simple and honest response like this one will do the trick:

I'm not ready to say, "I love you" yet.

A conversation will follow in which you'll likely need to explain the following:

Will you ever be ready to say, "I love you?"
Why don't you feel the same way?
Do you still want to be together?

How many of those questions you'll need to answer will depend on how insecure your partner feels. Presuming you don't want to break off the relationship—something you've probably waited far too long to do if you find yourself in this situation—honest answers should make your significant other feel much more significant.

Will you ever be ready? Yes, but only when you feel in love. You don't want to just say the words, you want to mean them as well.

Why don't you feel the same way? You'll need to provide a personal answer to this question. Regardless, reiterate that you care about your partner and want to feel in love with them in the future—you just don't feel that way right now.

Do you still want to be together? Yes. Unless you don't, in which case you should've said something before your partner dropped the love bomb. If this is the case, you need to end the relationship and stop stringing along your soon-to-be partner.

DON'T COMPENSATE FOR THE TRUTH

Not loving your partner can incite guilt, and that can lead you to act in ways that hurt both you and your partner. You don't want to act like John and end up asking Helen to move in with you. You'll want to provide ways to make your partner feel more at ease and closer to you, but resist that urge when it involves progressing your relationship too quickly. Nothing will speed your way to a bitter end like forcing yourself into something unprepared.

You shouldn't feel guilty for what you don't feel. You can't blame yourself if your partner feels hurt in this situation. That will happen no matter what you do, so as long as you remain honest and try to keep things positive, you should avoid offering any consolation prizes for a lack of love. Don't move in. Don't make promises you can't keep. Don't exaggerate other positive feelings you have. Many of these efforts will backfire—in many cases, immediately. You can never expect an easy relationship, and this challenge may present itself. If you want to remain with your partner and work towards love, you have to tell the truth.

ASKING FOR AN OPEN RELATIONSHIP

People suck at monogamy. With 41 percent of married couples admitting to adultery from one or both partners and more than half of both sexes confessing to at least one infidelity in their relationships*, you'll likely encounter a cheat at some point. For some, monogamy just isn't the answer.

Chlora started masturbating at age five. She didn't understand it until she got older, but she incorporated it into her young lifestyle. Chlora loved to play pretend shopping at home. Her mother would provide a $10 bill, and Chlora would go around the house asking how much certain items were. Items like zucchinis, cucumbers, candlesticks, spatulas, dog bones, and several other cylindrical items were her favorite purchases. She'd carefully pick a new selection each week, pay her mom, take all of her items back to her room, and take turns sticking them in her vagina. One week she concentrated her "purchases" on vegetables so much that mom required her to return them later that evening to make a salad for a dinner party. Chlora never shared what she did with them.

Her insatiable sexual appetite followed her throughout life. In college, her boyfriends complained about having sex too much. She told stories about weekends she'd spent in her apartment, repeatedly bouncing on her boyfriend only to take a break to cook him a panfull of bacon before going at it again. Chlora took so much out of her boyfriends that they temporar-

*Journal of Marital and Family Therapy (September 9, 2012): http://tinyurl.com/769z5dz.

ily lost the ability to ejaculate. She was insatiable. Nevertheless, she stayed monogamous. This was inconvenient, because individual boyfriends could never satisfy her and routinely broke up with her due to her incredible sexual demands.

Finally, she met a guy who knew of her legendary voracious appetites. His high sex drive seemed like a match, but even her needs outpaced his. In a bout of genius, he proposed an open relationship. When Chlora needed more sex, she could go get it. He, on the other hand, would stay home and watch television with an ice pack between his legs.

One afternoon he came over to surprise Chlora on her birthday, only to find her legs spread around a man in a donkey costume. Mr. Donkey hastily retreated, left Chlora and her boyfriend to talk, and things seemed fine. As time went on, however, Chlora's boyfriend couldn't get the image out of his mind. He had nightmares about her getting banged by a piñata. Aside from the disturbing imagery, what bothered him the most was that she had kept a part of herself from him. Chlora explored a fetish with someone else instead of going to her boyfriend, and that eventually led to the end of their relationship. Had they both set rules in advance, however, an open relationship could have worked out for the best.

KNOW YOUR MONOGAMY (OR LACK THEREOF)

When a couple decides on an open relationship, that doesn't mean monogamy goes out the window. Instead, it turns the restrictive rules of monogamy into more of a sliding scale. On one end, both partners maintain emotional and physical bonds with only each other. On the other end, they can maintain those same bonds with whomever they please. When a relationship becomes open, couples don't have to pick between those options. They can choose just about any place in between.

Let's discuss the differences. Sexual non-monogamy means at least one member of a couple can go outside of the relationship to meet his sexual needs. How far he can go depends on the rules they set up—something we'll get to in a bit—but still requires emotional and social monogamy. That means both parts of the couple seem completely monogamous to the outside world—they're just not in the bedroom. Polyamory, on the other hand, allows one or more members of the relationship to actually date other people. In most cases, polyamorous couples have primary relationships to establish a set of boundaries with other secondary or tertiary partners. Both situations vary quite a bit depending on what any particular couple decides. If you want an open relationship, you first have to choose where you fall on the spectrum and where you think your partner will as well.

TALK TO YOUR PARTNER

Open relationships don't just happen—they take a lot of effort to establish. Obviously you need to bring up the idea with your partner before you jump right in; otherwise, you're opting for infidelity. That talk can go a number of different ways depending on how your partner feels. Nevertheless, you have to cover the same essential points:

- *You have sexual needs the relationship can't meet.*
- *You want to open up the relationship to meet those needs.*
- *You want to discuss a way to do this that will make both parties satisfied.*

Just in case the list doesn't indicate this immediately, you shouldn't just go outside your relationship because you think your partner won't indulge a kink. Don't resort to non-monogamy unless you can't get what you want from a single partner. That may mean you just want to sleep with other people but still commit to one person in every other way. It also may mean your partner just can't get into your foot fetish and you want to find someone to only help you with that. Whatever the circumstances, don't jump straight to an open relationship if you can get what you want without one.

If an open relationship fits well for your situation, talk to your partner. He can always say no, but stay respectful and find ways to compromise. Don't expect to get everything you want. In fact, don't expect that your partner will sign off on sexual non-monogamy right away. Your other half may feel comfortable opening the relationship in the future but wants you to remain monogamous for the time being for a variety of reasons. If you just had a kid, you probably aren't getting a ton of sex and opening up your relationship is just plain irresponsible. You end up leaving your partner at home to deal with your child while you get to go out and have a good time.

Other life changes can make a partner want to keep things closed, too. Perhaps he just got a new job and can't give you the attention you are used to receiving for a couple of months while adjusting to the job. That may be the result of an insecurity, but it is nevertheless a temporary one. He may also just want to see that you will commit to him for a few months or years before letting you sleep with others. If you can't meet these kinds of demands and put in the work necessary to keep an open relationship going, you don't have what it takes to be a part of one.

All of that said, your partner may like the idea. He or she may want to seek sexual activity elsewhere as well. No matter what you expect, you never really know what you'll get until you ask. While you're in for an awkward conversation in the beginning, you might end up with a great reward by the end.

DEFINE OPEN

Chlora and her boyfriend screwed up here more than anywhere else. If you don't set up rules, essentially anything goes, and you can wind up finding your boyfriend and/or girlfriend riding a donkey in ways you never imagined. Nobody loves rules, but openness complicates relationships significantly in a culturally monogamous society. If you want release from those sexual confines, you need to set some rules and stick to them.

The rules you and your partner choose depend on what you want. Both partners need to have veto rights to any activity or situation. Overly restrictive rules will obviously defeat the purpose, but that's the sort of thing you need to hash out together. Many couples like to reserve certain activities just for themselves—or at least for when they're together, be it with a third person or not. For some, that's full-blown intercourse. For others, it's kissing. What you and your partner want to keep on and take off the table depends on your individual and mutual needs, but you can start by considering the following:

- *Whether or not to make it a polyamorous or just a sexually non-monogamous relationship*
- *Which sexual activities to allow*
- *Where these activities can take place*
- *When these activities can take place*
- *Which people are off limits (e.g., friends, strangers, etc.)*
- *If your partner wants to know about your sexual exploits, and vice-versa*
- *How you plan to remain safe (Don't forget about potential STDs!)*
- *Whether or not you can meet people online through a profile that other people might see*
- *How much you will keep a secret from friends (and even family)*
- *What to do if a problem occurs and how you'll revise the rules accordingly (e.g., one partner gets jealous, contracts an STD, etc.)*

When making the rules, you can discuss any potential aspects of the soon-to-be-open relationship. The more detail you get into, the better you can account for potential problems. Throughout the experience—especially in the beginning—keep the lines of communication open so you don't risk ruining the bond between you and your partner. Open relationships can create growth, but they can also cause a number of problems. It all depends on your approach as a couple and if you can maintain the honesty and trust necessary to make it work.

BREAKING UP

Relationships often end in one of two ways: both parties engage in a rational but emotional conversation, or at least one half of the terminal relationship loses his shit. Nobody really enjoys either scenario; but if you approach breakups with a level head, you'll avoid more of the awkwardness, anger, and hurt that often follows the death of romance.

After nearly a year together, Ben planned to ask Josephine to move in with him. He found a large apartment with all the things she liked, had lots of ideas for the future, and took her to her favorite restaurant to share it all with her. Before he had a chance to ask, Josephine told him she planned on taking a three-month road trip with her friends and dashed Ben's hopes for their relationship.

On the way to dinner, Josephine mentioned a cat. Ben had never met her cat, but they spent more time at his place than hers and wondered if he somehow missed it. In a strange ploy to get her to stay in town, he jokingly threatened to kidnap the cat. Josephine told him she didn't know where the cat was, and neither did her parents, so he'd have a tough time pulling that off. Frustrated, Ben suggested the cat just ran away and got eaten by a coyote. Josephine started to cry, and Ben quickly came to learn that's exactly what happened.

Josephine believed her cat saved her life. At seventeen, she wanted to die but thought her cat talked her out of it. She decided to overdose on pills, put them in a bowl, went to clean herself up, and found on her return that the cat had eaten them. It stumbled out of the window and ran off into the night, only to attract the attention of a few hungry coyotes.

Ben couldn't have known the history of Josephine's cat, but his "joke" brought up too many awful memories. She walked out of the restaurant, Ben tossed money on the table, and he went after her. She refused to talk the entire way home until she finally let him have it. Josephine never wanted to see him again and ended their relationship on the street.

REMEMBER THE GOOD THINGS

Relationships can end for a number of reasons. More often than not you make a rash decision in a fit of anger like Josephine did, decide you just don't like your partner anymore, or feel that you can't get what you need. Regardless of your emotional starting point, you want to stay calm and avoid the messy breakup. Remembering the good things—the things that made you want a relationship with your soon-to-be ex in the first place—can help you do that.

When you get angry or frustrated with your partner, you tend to temporarily wipe the good memories away. This makes it very easy to justify poor communication. You let yourself believe, at least subconsciously, that the person receiving your insults deserves them. You'll most likely feel differently once you've calmed down and regret the things you said, so better to start from a calm place before you hurt your partner unnecessarily. Before you approach the breakup conversation, make a mental list of what you like about your partner. If you really want to call it quits, don't use this information to convince yourself otherwise but simply remember that you don't hate him. You might feel a little sad about the breakup, but you should. Anger, on the other hand, doesn't belong.

GET TO THE POINT

Nobody enjoys getting dumped, so don't waste time and get to the point. Tell your partner clearly and don't spend minutes building up to the awful news.

> **DON'T DO THIS:** *Listen, Ben, we need to have a talk. I'm not really happy with the way things have been going and how you've been treating me. What you said about my cat really hurt and I don't think I can forgive you. I can't see you as anything other than a cat hater, and I can't be with a cat hater. What I'm trying to say is . . . I think we should break up.*

DO THIS: *I've given this a lot of thought, and I want to break up.*

In the bad example, Ben gets a lot of explanation that gives him ample time to freak out about what could come next. Furthermore, the actual breakup line comes off as very indecisive. When you end a relationship, don't say you think it should end. When you want something to stop, say so explicitly. It may seem a little harsh, but when you tell your partner you think something should end, that gives him hope that he can argue the opposite.

In the concise, good example, Ben gets two important messages: the decision didn't come lightly and the relationship is over. Conversation can then follow with the message clearly understood.

ASK QUESTIONS

When you end a relationship, you owe your partner some sympathy. He may agree with your decision or he may want to fight it. Either way, you should plan about an hour to talk with them. You might not need that much time, but better to play it safe when you have to hurt someone you care about.

You want to gear the conversation towards his feelings and thoughts. You can share how you feel as well, but spend more time asking questions and listening. Find out how he feels, show that you still care about him despite the breakup, and hear what he has to say. If he insults you or complains, just respond calmly and ask why he feels that way. When people get hurt, they might respond with anger and say things they don't mean. If you ask them to think about what they've said, they might realize the irrationality of the comment and apologize.

You want to get your partner to think as much as possible during this conversation and understand, logically, why the relationship had to come to an end. Emotion more than has its place in the conversation, but pure emotion doesn't create a productive environment. You can add a little logic to the situation by asking questions as well. If your partner wants you to explain why you want to break up, let him know that you'd like to hear what he thinks first. This gives him the opportunity to consider what he did wrong in the relationship and why it led to the breakup. That way, when you provide your answers your partner will better understand why you feel the way you do.

That said, don't answer every question with a question. If you do this, you'll come across as condescending and avoidant. You need to provide your partner with some answers or you'll frustrate him, so save the questions for moments when you need him to really think.

MAKE A PLAN

When you call it quits, make sure you talk about the future as well. Do you want to remain friends or not? How will you do that? How will you both move forward? While you don't have to iron out every detail the moment the relationship comes to a close, you should figure out the next steps so you don't separate and worry about it later.

Presuming you want to stay friends, plan to see your ex a week later just to hang out and talk. This gives you both time to process what happened and discuss everything after reality sinks in. During this conversation you can iron out some of the complicated details, like whether or not you want to know when the other starts dating again and how you plan to transition into a friendship. Some people will need time apart before they can see each other as friends again, and others can start that phase right away. Regardless, it will always feel a little weird and you both will need time to adjust. Take it slow, talk about how you feel when you need to, and eventually friendship will feel normal.

No matter how much you plan for a breakup or how many you've experienced in the past, it will always hurt more than you expect. No advice or strategy can take away the pain of lost love, but if you handle a breakup well you can minimize your heartbreak.

GETTING YOUR EX
TO BACK OFF

Sometimes love dies. What once made you feel better than anything now just looks like a turd heating up on the sidewalk. You can't make friendships out of every failed romance, and some ex-partners don't understand that. To get them to back off, you often have to assume the role of the bad guy or girl.

Olive couldn't go on without resolution. At age eight, she lost a tattered stuffed parrot and spent six weeks plastering posters all over her neighborhood, hoping someone would locate it. Eventually she learned that it fell behind the toilet, her father accidentally peed on it, and then he decided to throw it out without an explanation. Like most of the men in Olive's adult life, he learned that his daughter doesn't know when to stop.

Ben met her at an arcade bar (a "barcade") while playing a terrible game of Pac-Man. They dated for awhile, Ben learned about Olive's horrible temper, and the short relationship ended with a clean but explicit cut. At least, that's what Ben thought until the text messages started to roll in.

ONE WEEK

hi ben, do u know what time costco closes on saturday?

ONE MONTH

the woot sale is a two slankets for 8 bucks, thought you might want to know.

TWO MONTHS

hey ben, how have you been? what's new jew?

THREE MONTHS

so ben, i know you may not want to stay in touch with me but i genuinely would like to be your friend.

SIX MONTHS

hi ben, i got a viewsonic g-tablet. i was wondering if u could please help me with rooting it. i don't want to brick it & i really dont know what I'm doing.

ONE YEAR

hey ben, was just wondering if you wanted to meet up and have sex sometimes . . . let me know.

TWO YEARS

can i come over and cuddle?

THREE YEARS

i bought u a double rainbow shirt. do you still live in the same apartment?

Ben never responded to a single message, but they never stopped coming. When an ex-partner won't back off, you can't always assume time will solve your problem.

START WITH KINDNESS

An attached ex won't always get the picture during an angry breakup. While you might say you never want to see her again or come close to that, we all know how fury we felt one evening can subside or turn into a regret. An ex can reasonably assume that "I never want to see you again" could change with a few well-timed apologies.

If time passes and you still don't want to see your ex, you need to reiterate your feelings clearly. When you use even mildly wishy-washy language, you provide a loophole without realizing it. Because your ex wants you in her life again, she'll find hope in most any statement. In many cases, even a clear expression of your feelings won't do the job because you could always change your mind. That said, you should take the road of kindness—as much as possible, anyway—before you resort to harsher punishment.

> **DON'T DO THIS:** *I don't think I can be around you anymore. You were really mean to me and I don't want that in my life.*
> **DO THIS:** *I understand that you're sorry and I accept your apology, but I don't want you in my life anymore. I do not want you to contact me in any way.*

For some, a clear statement works. It helps if you forgive her, even if you don't feel she deserves it, because that can help provide closure for both of you. Swallow your pride and tell her that you accept her apology, regardless of how you feel. Your actions will speak volumes, and she'll know that you won't see her again because of what she did. If she argues, stand firm and do not waver from your message. You can always end the call if she won't stop arguing.

END WITH CRUELTY

You should never hurt someone else if you can help it, emotionally or otherwise. That said, some ex-partners may never get the message and won't back off until you make them feel they should. When logic fails in these situations, you have to resort to a minimal amount of cruelty.

In Ben's case, Olive wouldn't stop sending messages for three years. Ben should've confronted the situation right away, but he learned how aggressive an attached person can act when she wants a continued relationship or at least more closure. After polite attempts to solve the problem, he learned that only a little cruelty could do the trick:

> You have to stop contacting me. I do not want to talk to you, see you, or have you in my life in any way. I do not like you or care about you. If you continue to contact me, I will consider it harassment and take the appropriate measures to make sure you cannot contact me again in the future.

A little hurt can make your ex-partner dislike you enough to want to leave you alone. You can block her on your phone and email in some cases, but it helps to deal with the situation head-on so you know she won't trouble you further. If you block an ex, she may escalate her attempts and show up at your home or find you elsewhere. Don't take the risk just to avoid confrontation. End the situation so you don't find yourself in far worse circumstances.

PART V

SEX

Sex is awkward. It should be awkward. Most people take two sets of geni-tals, stick tab A into slot B, and hope for the best. Even if you go in with book knowledge on the subject, you learn a lot more through experience. If you want to have sex—and you really do—you have to power through the uncom-fortable moments. You can't stop them, but you can make them easier by taking the right approach.

Most people encounter problems because they don't talk about what they want. If you've long-held a desire to make love to the physical manifestation of a cartoon duck, you might have a harder time bringing that up. If you only want some instruction from your partner on the specifics of what he likes, or want to provide the same to him, you have an easier job. Still, most people like bedroom activities to fall into place and run into problems because of it. While some get lucky and require minimal verbal communication with their partner, most of us have to speak up to get what we want.

Awkward sex doesn't just stop at the mouth. With men (and even some women) involved, you can expect flying ejaculations at the very least. Sex gets messier due to a variety of bodily malfunctions and poor hygiene, lead-ing to many gross and surprising problems. It's important to handle them responsibly, but also to know when to stop because you or your partner has become too uncomfortable.

Sex helps us forget about the many icky things our bodies do to us and we do to them. Nobody objectively wants to lick a butt, but we'll try it and even love it under the right circumstances. In order to have great sex, you must remain open to some pretty gross stuff and really uncomfortable situations. They will inevitably happen, but this chapter will prepare you for the worst.

TALKING ABOUT HUMAN SEXUAL INTERCOURSE

Naked people, bodily fluids, and strange noises: if it didn't come with a great reward, a lot of people would avoid sex altogether. It's one thing to convince someone to sleep with you; it's another thing to have great sex. Opening a dialogue about what each person wants will help you get where you want to be.

Tessa and Justin had a great time on their first date. However, when they first kissed, he rammed his tongue down her throat and sucked on her lips, imitating the motions of a dental dry vacuum. She wasn't a fan of this, but didn't want to insult him by bringing it up. She tried to influence his tongue to act in less violent ways and concentrated on his charming personality.

While they were having sex for the first time, Justin expressed that he preferred the backdoor entry. Tessa was uncomfortable with the idea because she had never done it but also because she had a hemorrhoid. She wasn't sure what a penis might do to it and was too embarrassed to bring it up. Eventually, she opted to stop seeing him instead of having a conversation about what worked and didn't work for her.

CREATE A SAFE ZONE

Talking about sex can be difficult. Some people have fantasies or fetishes that they want to bring up, but they were judged in the past and are afraid of being judged again. Others don't feel comfortable talking about sex because of how they were raised. When you choose to initiate this conversation, you'll want to create a positive environment. Perhaps your motivation is to share what you enjoy, but if you're a good partner, you'll want to hear the other person's preferences as well. Make it clear that you won't criticize what your mate shares. The talk serves to create more trust and improve the level of intimacy in the relationship. Ensuring that your partner feels cared for should help him understand the importance of this conversation.

START WITH BABY STEPS

The first step in doing this is a preliminary conversation. Pick a time when neither of you are rushed or busy and a place where you won't get interrupted. Mention that you want to talk about your sexual relationship before you get into any meaty details. Some people will respond positively and appreciate that you took the first step. Others may feel shy or put on the spot. Use this time to find out how comfortable your partner feels with having a sex talk. If he feels awkward about it, talk about that, and why it's the case. Acknowledging that it's a difficult thing to discuss helps lift some of the pressure. Furthermore, how open he is will reveal a lot about his level of emotional security with you. If he doesn't want to talk about sex, it's likely that there are other aspects of his life or your relationship that he isn't talking about. If this is the case, you may have to have several conversations before you actually get to the one about what they enjoy sexually. Everyone moves at a different pace, and it's better to take some time with this now and create a trusting bond.

HAVE THE TALK

Once the initial conversation happens, both people should feel emotionally safe enough to actually talk about their sexual preferences. This could be the same day or several weeks later. When you get there, make sure it's still a two-way conversation. Both parties should be asking questions and sharing things about themselves. Use strength-based comments to talk about what you desire.

> **BAD:** *I wish you would blow me more often.*
> **GOOD:** *I really enjoy oral sex. Would you be open to doing it more often?*

If you make your partner feel good about what he's already doing, he should be excited to try new things with you. For instance, Justin was really good with his hands. Tessa could have started with that before discussing what she didn't like about his kissing style.

Even if the talk goes smoothly, don't stop there. Make it known that there's an open line of communication between the two of you, and that you both should keep sharing their feelings in and out of the bedroom.

While talking about sex can feel awkward, awkward sex feels worse. Whether you've been married for ten years or just started seeing someone, get over the uncomfortable hump and move on to better lovemaking.

NEGOTIATING A "FRIENDS WITH BENEFITS" SITUATION

Friends are fun. Sometimes they're more fun when you get to have sex with them. While that might seem like a relationship, the modern age invented a wonderful new middle ground: friends with benefits. Finding this elusive compromise between buddies and romantic partners takes work, and if you don't plan ahead you'll encounter problems along the way.

Nathan worked more than anyone he knew, to the point at which he barely slept, saw friends, or ate. Some mornings, if he woke up early enough, he'd conjure up some Internet pornography, enjoy a quick viewing session, and then microwave a breakfast burrito. Otherwise, Nathan launched straight into his work and didn't bother meeting any of his other needs. Some saw him as diligent and impressive. Others looked at Nathan as a sad recluse who'd wind up an old man with a sex robot that fulfilled his physical needs but inched him towards isolation-driven madness. As his unbecoming future weighed on his heart, Nathan figured a friends–with–benefits situation would temporarily bandage the wound without upsetting his work-centric lifestyle.

He hopped onto a variety of online sites, posted a few ads, and sorted through the replies. While many seemed either too timid or too risky, he finally found Martin, a man who appeared to suit his needs. They both worked a lot, had little time for romance, wanted semi-regular sex with an actual human, and didn't want to have said sex with someone they didn't know or care about at all. After exchanging a few messages, Nathan met

Martin at a coffee shop to see if they hit it off. They liked each other well enough and decided to go back to Martin's apartment.

They soon arrived, kissed, and everything felt right. Martin started to slip off Nathan's clothing, piece by piece, and kissed each part of his body. He led him into the bedroom, told him to wait, and came back with a small box. "I think it'd be really hot if you let me wax your body," Martin said. Nathan didn't want to abruptly part with his body hair but felt rude saying no and decided to let Martin try. Halfway through a wax, Nathan decided he couldn't take it anymore and put a stop to the festivities. He left Martin's apartment sporting half an Amish-style beard below the belt.

When you want a friend with benefits, don't rush in. Take the time you need to set up a healthy arrangement or you might lose your hair—figuratively and, possibly, literally.

HAVE A SEXLESS FIRST MEETING

Friends with benefits works better when you get to know the person you're going to sleep with before you sleep with him. If you have an existing friend in mind, great! If you're trying to meet someone new, hang out at least once without putting sex on the table. If you plan to carry on with this pseudo-relationship for awhile, you'll have plenty of time to sleep together in the future.

Meeting up first gives you the opportunity to decide whether or not you actually want to sleep with someone or if the attraction doesn't exist in real life. Again, if you have a friend in mind, you'll already know. If you don't and have to find someone new, you have time to decide if you really want to move forward or not. If you get asked to go back to his or her place right after meeting, you have to make a split-second decision you might regret. While you can't ensure you'll have a great time in the sack together, you can minimize the chance of an uncomfortable experience if you don't rush into one.

CREATE A GAME PLAN

After you meet up for the first time, you should decide how you want to proceed. While some people may want to jump right into it, and that can work, others may want to ease their way in. A friends with benefits situation should work like a relationship but without any commitment, so if you don't go straight to intercourse with someone you date you shouldn't here, either.

You can start with just kissing and see how you feel, then make your way around the bases as comfort dictates. It helps to know how you want to progress so you can stay on the same page with your special new friend. Even without the relationship, you still need to communicate effectively. Let's take a look at a sample plan:

- *If you don't know your special friend yet: meet up a few times to get to know each other.*
- *Outside of the bedroom, kiss first and see how things go. Depending on your comfort levels you may choose to wait until a later time to engage in and kind of sex.*
- *Take the first step into the bedroom and concentrate on genital-free foreplay. Keep the underwear on until both parties feel comfortable taking it off and verbally agree to do so. If you or your friend feels uncomfortable with moving forward, you can always stop. If you both want to take the next step, restrict this time to non-penetrative sex to avoid rushing into things.*
- *Full speed ahead!*
- **OPTIONAL:** *Try out any kinks or other sexual interests you or your special friend may have.*

You can set the pace according to your comfort level. Some people may feel fine moving quickly and skipping steps while others will need to go through the aforementioned list at a snail's pace. Only you can know what feels right for you, so progress as you and your special friend see fit.

KNOW THE RULES

Friends with benefits situations don't come with a societally prescribed set of rules to follow—you have to make them up yourself. When you get into a pseudo-relationship with a buddy, hash out the terms beforehand. To start, you should discuss the following:

- *Is this an exclusive situation, or can we mess around with other people?*
- *If we mess around with other people, do we need to disclose? (Remember, this may not matter for emotional reasons but can have an impact on your physical safety—don't discount the impact of STDs!)*
- *How often should we expect to get together?*
- *Will we just have sex most of the time, or will we also hang out and do "friend stuff" without the sex?*

- Will we ever hang out with other people or keep this pseudo-relationship to ourselves?
- What do we do if one person develops feelings for the other? (More on this later.)

It also helps to know what is and isn't on the table:

- Will we explore any fetishes or kinks together?
- Will we incorporate toys into our sexual activity?
- Do we want to invite others into the bedroom occasionally or often?
- Does either person have an aversion to certain practices (e.g. doggie style, grabbing hair, facials, light biting, licking armpits, etc.)?

Beyond that, you should discuss how you like to have sex and what feels good. You can do this during sex, and even masturbate together to learn what kind of touches you both enjoy. This can seem like a lot, but don't approach it like a sexual inventory. You can make an arousing experience out of talking about what you enjoy. Get descriptive, and it can make those first couple of meets build up to a hot first time when you finally get into bed together.

MANAGE YOUR FEELINGS

While a lot of advice for friends with benefits situations can apply to a relationship, you have to stay completely aware of the difference. When you have sex with a friend, you don't do it with the intention of falling in love or turning it into something serious. While you can't always resist your feelings—nor should you—you need to manage your expectations. When you find a friend with benefits, you undertake the relatively high risk of unrequited love.

Talk to your special friend about how you want to handle this situation. Even if both parties think no feelings will develop, the possibility still exists. In most every case you should disclose feelings when they arise and plan how to proceed. Do you want to end the arrangement if feelings develop? Do you want to talk about the possibility of upgrading to a relationship? You don't have to decide in advance, but it helps to acknowledge the possibility because emotions exist and you take a big risk if you deny them. When you spend a fair amount of time with someone and his genitalia, you can easily feel like you are in a relationship. Small checkups to see how you and your special friend feel about the relationship help a lot. You don't need huge amounts of regular communication—because that's relationship territory—but a little goes a long way.

Feelings create a bigger risk when you upgrade an existing friend to one with benefits. When you meet someone new and just get a "regular thing" going, you don't lose an established relationship if things go awry. You can make more mistakes with someone you meet for the purposes of friendship and sex than you can with someone whose friendship you already have. On the plus side, you probably communicate reasonably well with a friend. Make use of that, and acknowledge the risk you take by adding sex to the mix. If you discuss your circumstances regularly you can catch problems before they become unmanageable and have the capacity to ruin your friendship.

KNOW WHEN TO PUT ON THE BREAKS

Friends with benefits situations get complicated when feelings enter the mix, but other outside factors play a role as well. If you or your special friend meet someone you want to date, work makes it hard to spend much time together, a loved one becomes sick or dies, or any sort of life-changing event occurs, plan to put sex on hold.

Sex between friends works under the right circumstances but exists in a sort of limbo that you can easily disrupt with life changes. Before you jump into bed with a pal, discuss the possibility of putting things on hold when certain life events require your (or his) attention. Both parties need to understand that this arrangement can stop at any time for almost any reason—kind of like at-will employment for your genitals. If you remember to regard your sexual benefits as ephemeral, you reduce the risk of getting hurt if they suddenly screech to a halt.

HAVE FUN

You have a lot to think about when you pursue sex with a friend, but you can have a great time, too. Enjoy yourself and each other. Think of your special friend as someone who can help you learn more about what you enjoy in the bedroom. Sometimes these arrangements turn into relationships. More often they exist as flings. Either way, enjoy the time you have. It may not last forever, but that's sort of the point.

APPROACHING PORN IN A RELATIONSHIP

We like to look at beautiful people. Many of us like to look at beautiful people having sex with each other. Thanks to a lot of cultural norms, we don't get to feel this way without a little—and sometimes a lot—of shame, guilt, and jealousy thrown into the mix. So how can a relationship survive when porn gets involved? It can't without a specific brand of compromise.

Ben kept a very special hard drive tucked into the corner of his night-stand. He filled it with gigabytes of porn he aspired to watch someday. Thanks to Ben's bisexuality, it ranged from epic parodies like *Womb Raider* to the candid, no-nonsense *Balls Deep*. He spent a few nights each week picking out a new title, watching in bits and pieces, deliberating, and sorting it into a folder on his computer. This not only satisfied his sexual needs, but also his obsessive-compulsive tendencies. This small hobby seemed harmless until he became serious with his girlfriend, Josephine.

Josephine wanted the kind of simple, monogamous passion found in her favorite romance films. She thought of Ben's penis less as a sexual organ and more as a spiritual device to combine them into a single entity. When snooping one afternoon, she came across his porn drive. The meticulously sorted library shattered her romantic fantasy, and she confronted Ben so he could watch her destroy the drive. While you don't want to share every one of your sexual interests early in a relationship, you want to talk about porn before things get too serious. Ben and Josephine both made incorrect assumptions about each other, and it resulted in unnecessary disaster.

TALK TO YOUR PARTNER ABOUT PORN EARLY ON

Although not necessarily first-date material, you should know how your partner feels about porn before you get too deeply involved. Maybe you love it, hate it, or don't care about it at all; but you both need to accept each other's positions on the subject. At best, you'll find out you both don't need it or want to watch it together. At worst, you'll discover you may have a sexual incompatibility and come to a compromise. When you avoid this conversation, you and/or your partner may feel hurt when they discover your secret interests.

In Josephine's case, she felt betrayed because Ben seemingly spent quite a bit of time meticulously archiving porn of many varieties. He acquired titles en masse and often didn't know the specific contents of what he downloaded, but Josephine looked at a few and came to the erroneous conclusion that he secretly wanted to tie her up and pee in her mouth. Conversely, Ben didn't realize Josephine's deeply romantic fantasies because she'd never mentioned them. He assumed they were just having sex, but she was imagining something out of a romance novel instead. Both parties failed to disclose and discuss their interests, so the sex they thought they were having suddenly became something else entirely.

Failing to discuss sexual interests causes this kind of misunderstanding—the kind that you can easily avoid with a quick conversation. All you have to do is bring up the topic and speak honestly while listening to what your partner has to say. Avoid aggressive opinions if you disagree and try to come to a compromise that works for both of you.

> **DON'T DO THIS:** *I want to talk about porn. I watch it a lot, and I want you to know that I'm going to keep watching it even though we're dating. If you have a problem with it, you need to learn to deal with it.*
> **DON'T DO THIS:** *I want to talk about porn. I don't like it, and I don't want you to watch it. If you can't give up porn for me, we can't be in a relationship.*
> **DO THIS:** *I want to have a conversation about porn. It's something I (do/ don't) enjoy, but I know that's not how everyone feels so I want to figure out how it fits into our relationship.*

This conversation should lead to a healthy compromise, but sometimes you'll find yourself romantically involved with another human who doesn't share your feelings on the subject. If you want to maintain a relationship with someone who won't allow you this pleasure, you only have a few options: do what your partner wants, continue to look at porn and lie about it, or try to find a tolerable compromise that requires more sacrifice than you'd prefer. While your partner's aversion to pornography may feel unreasonable, you have to decide if his prolonged company is worth your sacrifice—a sacrifice that has a lot more to do with your personal freedoms than it does with what you're giving up.

KNOW THE PROBLEMS PORN CAUSES

Porn can cause serious problems and your partner may have a legitimate reason to request its dismissal. The amount of porn Ben watched made it a frequent element of his sexual life. For some, that's fine. For others, it can cause performance issues in real-world sex. When you get used to beautiful people pounding away at one another using a variety of unrealistic methods, you can find that more arousing than an actual person. Just as *Sesame Street's* Cookie Monster discovered that cookies are a sometimes-food, porn needs to be a sometimes-orgasm. When you want the ability to appreciate the large spectrum of sexual pleasure, you need to diversify your interests.

Furthermore, porn offers an unrealistic depiction of sex that can lead to unfair expectations in the bedroom. While few of us will try to realize acts carried out in *Edward Penishands*, *Star Whores*, and the like, porn requires a variety of adjustments to the natural act of sex for film purposes. When we copulate normally, we don't expose our genitals for a camera. For the most part, we mash our bits together and enjoy the pleasure. In porn, actors must cheat to the camera and put themselves in unusual positions in order to capture their penetrative acts on "film." Also, porn seeks to depict both simple and complex fantasies. It often forgoes necessary foreplay, any necessary preparation, and the problems couples will regularly encounter during the act. On top of that you see sex that might look hot but feels completely different in actual practice. Add strange story and role-playing elements to the mix and you end up with a semi-polished product that edits out the complexity of sex. If you watch enough porn, it'll leave you with the wish of easily realizable desires and without the knowledge that pro-level sex doesn't just happen.

As a porn connoisseur, you also have a responsibility to consume responsibly. Hopefully it goes without saying that you should make masturbation a private practice and not involve unwilling spectators, but you should also manage where, when, and how you watch pornography. Ben did the right thing by keeping everything on a separate hard drive that he hid from the world. You don't want to save a bunch of porn to a hard drive in your computer or keep bookmarks right in your web browser. You need to maintain a barrier to discovery, even if you disclose your interest to others. At some point you may have kids in the house or visitors over for a party. If someone takes a computer break and comes across *Good Will Humping*, you're in for embarrassment. You may even expose a minor to something he shouldn't watch out of context or at all.

WITH GREAT PORN COMES GREAT RESPONSIBILITY

While relationships should allow for pornography consumption, both partners need to give a little when they disagree. Remember that porn is a sometimes orgasm, it doesn't depict reality, and can cause some very real issues in a relationship. That said, when used responsibly it can also provide a lot of fun.

DISCUSSING A WEIRD
BEDROOM QUIRK

Only a fair number of people have sexual fetishes—and we'll get to those later—but most of us have some weird sexual quirk. You might not realize it, and it may go unnoticed or ignored by some partners, but it's there. If your partner does something strange in bed that you don't like, do yourself and him a favor by talking about it.

When Josephine first stuck Ben's dick in her mouth, she approached the situation calmly and gently. She didn't love oral sex. She found it impersonal and kind of gross. However, she loved Ben, and Ben loved blow jobs, so she gave it the old college try. Like a good boyfriend, Ben reciprocated. With enough time, Josephine came to enjoy the act and approached it eagerly. One day she surprised Ben with a blow job and that eagerness created a very awkward situation.

Josephine decided to employ some tips she'd read on the Internet. Through a few errors in her performance combined with her unique biology, every sucking motion created a special noise. Ben felt as though he was receiving oral sex form a dying giraffe*, so it took no more than a few seconds for him to burst out laughing. Josephine didn't find the humor in her blow job and asked him what was so funny. He didn't tell her, claimed he got distracted, and asked her to continue. The noises persisted, Ben laughed a few more times, and Josephine left in a rage.

*http://tinyurl.com/dyinggiraffe

Had Ben simply told the truth or mentioned the strange noise before he laughed, he would have avoided hurting Josephine's feelings and losing out on an orgasm. When your partner does something strange in bed, confront the situation before it grows into a real problem.

TAKE A BREAK

You probably won't end up with a partner who sounds like a dying giraffe while administering oral sex, but you will encounter a strange incompatibility here and there. Some people really like to cuddle immediately while others like to clean themselves up first. According to a startling Consumer Habits study,* 20% of today's youth text during sex. You may even encounter the rare but very real post-sex flatulator. How many times will you allow someone to fart immediately after making love? Probably just once, and you'll want to address the situation immediately. You should treat every sexual quirk that way.

First things first, put any sexual activity on hold and talk to your partner. Don't approach the conversation like you have a huge problem you need to solve right now, but start off with a question:

Would you mind if I washed up before we cuddle?
Are you making a strange noise?
Are you aware that you fart immediately after sex?

It helps to start with how he perceives the situation and work your way forward from there. Maintain a polite tone, of course, as anything you say can sound accusatory when put the wrong way. Your partner may not know about his quirk or it may only bother you, so you want to avoid direct complaints. Questions help you to do that.

* http://www.jumio.com/2013/07/where-do-you-take-your-phone

DON'T ACCUSE

You can't talk about something someone else does without a little accusation, as you have to point to one of his actions as a problem, but you can reduce your aggression. Asking a question helps, but as you continue the conversation you should avoid negative statements like these:

You make weird noises when you blow me.
You do this disgusting thing immediately after sex.

Your partner probably doesn't know that you don't like what he's doing and might not even be aware of the problem. Give him the benefit of the doubt and take the blame out of your statements:

I'm not sure if it's you or me causing this, but when you blow me, I'm hearing some weird noises.

After we're done having sex, if we cuddle right away I get really messy and feel kind of gross. I need to clean up before I can do that; otherwise, I won't enjoy it.

The more you can make the statement about yourself and your needs, rather than a problem caused by your partner, the less awkward you'll both feel about the conversation. A good boyfriend or girlfriend won't mind a minor adjustment in the bedroom.

That said, in some cases—like with the farting—you may encounter a partner who has a problem he or she can't fix alone. In that case, you either decide to cope with the issue on your own or help him find a solution. If you want to cure him of his awful quirk, make sure you don't hurt him in the process. Let your partner know that you'll still like (or love) him if he can't fix the problem, but you'd like to try for your mutual benefit. If you can't find a fix, don't keep pushing it. You don't want to give your partner a complex over something he can't control.

You'll find that in most cases you can fix the problem either through conversation or with a little work. Just don't leave any sexual quirks alone for too long. You run the risk of insult if you wait, but you can fix the problem while still small if you nip it in the bud.

TALKING ABOUT FETISHES

Nothing puts an abrupt end to a budding romance like asking your date to suck the mucus out of your nose. Whether you want to indulge in nasolingus or any other fetish, revealing your secret desire requires a little planning and tact if you don't want to get dumped.

Toby was a tall Swedish man with too much love to give. He saw a lifelong partner in every date, quickly shared personal details some couples hide for years, and expected the same in return. He'd do anything for his lovers, and never neglected an opportunity to bring a personalized gift. If you liked tulips, he'd bring you tulips. If you hated flowers altogether, he'd bring you bags of corn flour as a joke. He also loved unprotected sex, and inserted his penis into any willing hole with no regard for what came before. To Toby, this meant trust. To a more practical and vigilant population, this meant STDs. He was thoughtful and catered to his dates' specific needs, expecting the same in kind. Specifically, he wanted his partner's feet and calves clothed in sweaty rainbow socks. In the throes of lovemaking, he'd hold one foot flat against his nose so he could snort the scent on his path towards physical bliss. And while some lovers were willing to indulge his behavior, his habit of being a bit too upfront about this predilection needlessly alienated many of them. We often meet people like Toby who appear charming but betray our expectations because they ask too much too quickly. When you need to tell your partner about a fetish, pick the right time.

A TIME FOR EVERY FETISH

When choosing the right time to share your fetish with your partner, consider its general popularity. Many people have foot fetishes, but fewer want to become adult babies. You can roll out the truth sooner if you have a more common, well-accepted fetish because it won't seem as strange to as many people. Never wait too long, however, because your partner may feel deceived.

HOW WEIRD IS YOUR FETISH?

Let's take a look at some fetishes, from light to extreme, to get an idea of where yours might fall.

═══════════════════ **LIGHT** ═══════════════════

PODOPHILIA	Podophiles are foot fetishists, so don't confuse them with pedophiles! They enjoy feet in a sexual context and like to sniff, rub, lick, and suck on them.
BDSM	BDSM is an acronym for *bondage, discipline, sadism,* and *masochism,* a group of fetishes that are often grouped together. Many people have a light interest in BDSM, and some have a more extreme interest. If you just like to get tied up or tie your partner up in a little light bondage, you can suggest this fetish pretty early on. The more extreme your BDSM interests go, the more you might want to wait.
FAT FETISHISM	Not everybody loves a thin, fit body. The sexual desire for larger people runs frequently through the erotic minds of many people.
UROLAGNIA	Also known as "golden showers," or just an interest in peeing/getting peed on for sexual gratification, pissing on someone's face and/or body brings a lot of joy to people around the world. Fortunately, pee is sterile so this is a pretty safe fetish.
EXHIBITIONISM	Although many people look at exhibitionists as people who like to expose themselves in public to an unknowing population—and those people certainly exist—most people just like to have sex in a semipublic place (e.g. a bathroom, movie theater, etc.) due to the thrill of getting caught.
VOYEURISM	Some people just like to watch other people have sex or masturbate—but not necessarily their partner.

═══ INTERMEDIATE ═══

CUCKOLDISM People who like to experience, or at least know about, their partner having sex with another are cuckolds.

FORNIPHILIA A stranger and less common form of BDSM, forniphiles like to become furniture or be incorporated into furniture.

MENOPHILIA Menophiles enjoy watching a woman menstruate. Some enjoy licking maxi pads and sucking on tampons.

TAMAKERI Tamakeri, also known as "ball busting," involves abusing a man's testicles for his sexual pleasure. Tamakeri enthusiasts like a good kick in the balls.

OCULOPHILIA Some people enjoy oculolinctus, or licking eyeballs, as evidenced in Vladmir Nabokov's 1955 novel *Lolita*. Anything that gets in your eye can go straight into your bloodstream, so if you get an eyeball licked make sure isn't attached to an oral herpes carrier (or worse).

═══ EXTREME ═══

NASOLINGUS People who enjoy nasolingus either enjoy a tongue in their nose, their tongue in someone else's nose, or both. Sometimes this involves a little sucking—and, therefore, a little mucus—too.

VORAREPHILIA We all get hungry, but vorarephiles enjoy sexual gratification from eating people. Most people interested in *vore* don't actually want to eat a live person, but do like to fantasize and role-play such a scenario.

PARAPHILIC INFANTILISM Commonly known as adult babies, people with this fetish like to be treated like an infant, diapers and all. This fetish falls on the extreme side because of the amount of care required by the partner—including the changing of a shit-filled diaper.

OBJECTOPHILIA Objectophiles eroticize objects. While they can engage in relationships with a human, they may leave said human for the Berlin Wall or an iPhone.

You can share a foot fetish or light bondage shortly after becoming sexually active. With lesser-known and more complicated interests like nasolingus and vorarephilia, you should take enough time to develop a sexual rapport and an open line of communication in bed before you make your big reveal. Regardless of the time frame, you need to demonstrate to your partner that you can have and enjoy standard, vanilla sex. This will assuage any concerns that all future sex, following the disclosure of your fetish, will suddenly become strange and uncomfortable.

Because Toby wanted only sex with smelly rainbow-socked feet and made this known as soon as possible, he vastly limited the number of willing partners. When you disclose, you want to give your love interests enough time to know and care about you so you're not the guy or girl with the weird fetish but rather someone he likes who happens to have a kink.

PUT YOUR BEST FOOT FORWARD

Don't share your fetish like you'd share the results of a bad STD test. Tell your partner about your interests and focus on his advantages. A foot fetish can seem strange, but it also affords your partner frequent massages and compliments. The more rare nasolingus can help people suffering from sinus allergies. (This is not true, but rather a joke, and the suggestion helps to acknowledge the absurdity of a fetish and bridge the comfort gap between you and your partner.) Not all fetishes come with built-in benefits for new participants, but your partner may learn to love an unusual sex act once he gives it a few tries. If you can't sell any specific perks, you can sell that.

When you ask your partner to keep an open mind and try something in bed you enjoy, do right by him and offer the same in return. Let him know that you remain open to any sexual interests he may have now or develop in the future. A willingness to try new things keeps sex fun and exciting, even if that means you might masquerade as a piece of human furniture from time to time.

ACCIDENTALLY POOPING DURING SEX

Sex is messy, but most of the time you won't take an unexpected crap in the bed. Most of the time. Our bodies can betray us when things come out that we wish would stay inside. When that happens to you or your partner, handle it with grace.

Hygiene wasn't Olive's greatest skill, but she managed to keep clean and hide her eccentricities. She never ate a booger when she thought someone could see her. She didn't forget to flush the toilet on purpose. She chose not to shower after sex because she liked the memories the odor provided. Olive hid these qualities when she first went out with Ben, but on one fateful dinner date she gambled on a bean souffle and lost.

After a tasty meal, Olive brought Ben back to her place for a movie and it quickly evolved into sex. Despite gentle beginnings, Olive quickly made a request. She bent over and asked Ben to stand at the foot of the bed, grab her waist, and ravage her as hard as he wanted. Surprised and somewhat delighted, Ben obliged. They positioned themselves, as Ben placed his hands around her and started to pound away. Unfortunately, with just the right amount of pressure on her stomach, Olive squeezed out a liquid fart. Much like the last bit of ketchup in the bottle, a brown, watery explosion hit Ben's torso, neck, and chin with a slap. We all wipe our own poop away every day with a few dry squares of paper and think very little of it. However, when you combine someone else's shit, the element of surprise, and innate revulsion, you can expect a poor reaction. Ben shrieked like a child. Olive called him a pussy and threw a pillow at him. Neither party handled the situation well.

STAY CALM AND CARRY ON

Whether someone farts, queefs, pees, or poops on you during sex—and you didn't ask for it—you need to remain calm. As much as you might want to get out of this incredibly uncomfortable situation, you have to talk about what happened. You can't categorize accidental poop—during sex or otherwise—as deliberate. Neither of you wanted this moment to occur, and so when you ignore the moment, you make the mistake of judging your partner for a very embarrassing error.

When a body malfunction occurs, get cleaned up, table the sex for later, and talk about what happened. It's okay to let your partner know you didn't enjoy it—and assume she didn't either—but you also have to make it clear that you don't hate her for an unintentional error.

> **DON'T DO THIS:** *Ahhhhhhhhhhhhh! Grooossssssss!*
> **DO THIS:** *I'm sure you didn't mean for that to happen, so I'm not mad. I'm going to go get cleaned up, so let's stop the sex for now and talk about it so we don't have to feel really weird.*

While you might have planned a less crappy evening, how you handle a moment like this can make or break a bond between you and your partner. If you can get past an unappealing body malfunction and continue the relationship, you'll both gain the ability to be vulnerable with each other. Surviving hardships together strengthens a relationship, even if you seal that new foundation with literal feces instead of metaphorical glue.

APOLOGIZE

When your body releases an unwanted gas, liquid, solid, or any combination of the three, onto your partner you should apologize. Regardless of your intentions, you still just took a dump on someone else while you were having sex. If you accidentally hit someone's car, you would apologize. The same principle applies to body malfunctions.

That said, don't take any abuse from the wronged party. You didn't mean to poop during the throes of passion. You don't want to react like Olive and get angry, but you should defend your integrity (even though you may not feel like you have any left). If your partner treats you poorly, ask him to take a moment to calm down and realize that you didn't do anything maliciously or even intentionally. Give him time to relax—he deserves a few minutes to process what happened, after all—and then try to have a civil conversation about the event. Although disgusting, any rational person will understand that you didn't poop on him on purpose. From there, you can discuss practical ways to avoid the problem in the future.

REVERSE THE ORDER
While you may run into an unexpected fart from time to time—the easily forgivable body malfunction—you should try to avoid the problem as best you can. When you plan to have a meal that might impact your sex life, don't eat it before intercourse. Instead, have the great sex you want to have before you eat and then enjoy the meal when you and your partner have already achieved physical satisfaction.

KNOW YOUR BODY (AND, SPECIFICALLY, YOUR ANUS)
No human body works in the same way, but most people process foods similarly. Before you choose what to eat, you should know how your body will process the meal. For most people, significant amounts of red meat, coffee, beans, and vegetables cause gas. Foreign foods you don't commonly eat can cause indigestions because your body doesn't normally process them. You can find broad information about how your body will react to certain foods online, but you can learn a lot more by consulting a health professional. At your next visit to your doctor, discuss your diet and find out what you can eat to reduce your farting and pooping potential. While awkward for you, each and every body must excrete waste and gas on a regular basis. Doctors know this best.

If you have extreme reactions to certain foods, and body malfunctions happen to you on a frequent basis, you should work with your doctor to find the underlying problem. You may also want to visit a registered dietician to learn more about what you can eat so that you don't soil the bed on a regular basis.

As the boy scouts say, "always be prepared." While you'll rarely get a positive reaction when you accidentally spray paint your partner brown, you can lower your chances of causing a problem by using these suggested changes and by having an emergency poop plan in place.

THROWING SOMEONE OUT OF BED

Most people want to believe that they're masters of the bedroom, but few earn that very subjective title. More often, you end up with a partner who fails to meet your needs. Sometimes a simple adjustment can solve the problem. Other times you need to show him the door.

Ben invited Peter over to "hang out" with the tacit understanding that sex would take place. After a few sips of wine and sparse conversation, Peter decided to make a move. Some aggressive kissing raised no red flags, but soon Peter grabbed Ben's chest like he intended to rip it off. Ben yelped and complained several times before Peter stopped, at which point he commanded Ben between his legs. As Ben slowly complied, he found more than expected: genitals that bore the scent of a steamy volcano erupting with ass. Ben felt he'd had enough and told Peter they needed to stop immediately.

Peter found himself in a dilemma. As a reasonable fellow, he wasn't going to coerce Ben into anything he didn't want to do—however, Peter also wanted to have sex. Rather than forcing Ben to finish what they'd started, he just begged and begged. After Ben's several requests for Peter to get dressed and get out, Peter erupted into fury and trashed the apartment before finally taking his leave. Not all sex stinks quite like Peter and Ben's did; but in any case, when discomfort enters the mix, you shouldn't resort to politeness— you need to press pause and solve the problem before things become much, much worse.

COMMUNICATE FIRST

Most people don't like to talk during sex, unless, of course, someone appreciates fetishized erotic conversation. However, embellishing the physicality of the act doesn't really communicate anything about how you or your partner truly feels in the moment. Most humans approach sex with the idea that intuition will carry them through the experience. It won't, and clearly didn't with Ben and Peter. While some people just click, most need to work at making sexual experiences positive for everyone involved. It's important that you're confortable with your body and sharing it with another person before you engage in sexual activity. You don't want to throw someone out of bed just because you're generally uncomfortable with sex.

That means you have to talk to your partner—whether temporary or long-term—about what you like. Many of us feel too vulnerable to approach a conversation like this because it involves sharing intimate details of how we like to feel pleasure. Furthermore, people feel that the primal, visceral nature of the act disappears when you introduce a script or even an outline of what you want to do. Sometimes, yes, you lose a little bit of the element of surprise when you talk things out in advance; but you also gain the likelihood that your partner will give you what you want. As your sexual activity continues you won't need to discuss as much. When you learn what your partner likes and he learns the same of you, the sex will actually meet your needs and can still incorporate a few pleasant surprises here and there.

Because advance communication makes such a big difference, you need to make yourself comfortable with the idea of sharing your sexual interests. That discomfort doesn't only stem from the usual fears of vulnerability, but also because many of us don't know how to describe what we like (or don't even know in the first place). If you fear public speaking, you don't fear the crowd so much as you worry about screwing up in front of one. Preparing your material and knowing what you want to say alleviates the dread of a public speech. The same principle applies to talking about sex: if you spend some time getting to know what you like and describing it to yourself, you can easily describe it to your partner. If you don't masturbate, start. If you do, pay attention to how you do it and what makes you feel good. Next time you find yourself in a sexual encounter, use that information to inform your partner.

DON'T COMPLAIN! ASK FOR WHAT YOU WANT

When you talk about sex with a partner for the first time, don't do what Ben did with Peter. While it may seem like Ben was the victim of a hookup gone wrong, he didn't handle the situation well. He told Peter certain things hurt, and he didn't like what Peter did. At other times, he just allowed Peter to do whatever he wanted regardless of how it felt. Rather than expressing the problem, Ben let it boil up until he couldn't take it anymore before ending the festivities. Sometimes you just have to say no and put an end to the discomfort, but you don't want to start off with negative comments before you get there.

> **DON'T DO THIS:** *Stop grabbing my chest so hard, it hurts and feels like you're trying to rip it off.*
> **DO THIS:** *It hurts when you grab me like that, but I might like it if you were more gentle.*

When you give criticism in any situation—especially when in the bedroom—it helps to provide constructive feedback. You don't have to like everything, but you should know what you want instead. Figure that out and tell your partner so he or she can replace an activity you don't like with one that you do. When you end on a positive note—one that provides a helpful suggestion that will make sex better for all involved—you won't cause any bruised egos.

TRY A SOFT STOP FIRST

Despite your best attempts to resolve a sexual issue in the moment, sometimes you just need to take a break to formulate a new plan of action. Nobody likes to stop fooling around to talk instead, but when you have to pick between a short conversation and a night of miserable sex you should pick the conversation every time. You only need to do the following:

- *Gently ask your sexual partner to stop rubbing, sucking, kissing, or whatever the case may be.*
- *Let your partner know that you feel uncomfortable but want to fix that.*
- *Provide constructive suggestions to help your partner fix the problem.*
- *Get back to having sex.*
- *Give positive feedback. If your partner does something right, acknowledge it.*

You may not end up having the best sex of your life, but it's better to choose some pleasure over a lot of discomfort.

JUST SAY NO

When all else fails, just say no. Tell your sexual partner that you don't want to continue and he needs to get dressed. Nothing can erase the awkwardness of this situation, but that discomfort will fade much faster than the memory of awful sex you didn't want to have. Ben got this right. Unfortunately Peter felt the need to break every mirror in the apartment and flip over the kitchen table before accepting reality, but after calling it quits, most people will find themselves in just a small argument and not a battlefield of semen.

Say no politely, but with force. You don't want to solve the problem with malice, but clarity matters. Your soon-to-be-former sexual partner needs to understand that this will not continue and he's crossed a line. Make it clear that further sexual activity will not occur because you've left your comfort zone. Some people will argue. Others will apologize. Either way, prioritize your own comfort and not that of the person making you uncomfortable. When you want to stop, say so.

PART VI

FAMILY

Whether they like each other or not, your parents had sex at least once. Maybe your dad wanted to impregnate your mom for several months, or maybe he just forgot to use a condom. There are all kinds of parents—some abandon their children, some decide to birth an entire baseball team. Some realize that they are gay. Some only have one child and turn him into a spoiled brat. Some start meth labs in their basements. Some sing songs while escaping the Nazis. Some love each other and their kids very much and stay together happily ever after. Even in that case, the family will probably encounter a hiccup somewhere along the way. Or someone will die suddenly of an aneurism. These things happen.

Even if you love your family dearly, you have probably had issues with them at some point in your life. Maybe your parents never understood that you grew up and can handle things on your own. Or they force you to attend family events at which you have to talk to relatives you can't stand. Alternatively, they may seem distant. Sometimes parents get divorced and lose the ability to communicate with you and/or each other. Other times you're just not sure if you can ask them for help—especially if it's about subjects like sex.

When you leave the house, you can choose who you live with, who you date and who you hang out with. However, no one will ever replace your relatives. Even if you don't have much in common with them, you wouldn't exist if they hadn't created you. Whether you see your family every day or once every ten years, address the awkwardness you feel instead of shoving it under the rug. Remember that many seemingly irrational actions come from a place of love. Take advantage of the time you have with your family, because after all, they'll eventually be dead.

STAYING SANE DURING FAMILY EVENTS

Whether it's Christmas, the Fourth of July, or the annual dumpster diving party, you'll probably have to see your family at least once a year. Be assertive and honest about what you can handle so the entire thing isn't an uncomfortable mess.

Claire wasn't religious, but she enjoyed Christmas. The turkey, the Yule log, and the gift giving made her feel warm inside. One year, her parents—Frank and Michelle—decided to celebrate by getting divorced. Michelle and Frank somehow turned an argument over a gift into the end of a twenty-year marriage and Michelle decided to leave for good. However, the rest of the family was due to visit at any minute. While Michelle had no problem moving out, she couldn't say good-bye to the turkey she'd been carefully basting for eight hours. She finished her signature cranberry sauce and served her unsuspecting guests. Claire and her parents sat through the meal in excruciating silence while the rest of the family complimented Michelle on the moistness of her breast. The tension became so unbearable that she finally pretended to get called in to work, and the rest of the family took their Yule log to go. You might not be able to avoid a Christmas like Claire's, but you can find a way to survive most family events.

RELAX

A lot of us go into family events with emotional baggage. This means we're stressed or angry before we even see our relatives. Instead of agonizing over how awful the event might be, try to remain level-headed when you go into it. If someone brings up a touchy subject or asks you a question you don't want to answer, tell him you'll discuss it later. That'll at least give you time to process and figure out the most diplomatic way to deal with it. If your mom starts drinking too much or your uncle gets irrationally angry, try not to immediately let it get to you. Obviously this is easier said than done, but try to understand why these people do the things they do. Instead of criticizing your mom's drinking in front of everyone, talk to her about it when she's sober and approach it from a place of concern. Remember that if you're invited to a family function, it's because there's at least one family member who cares enough to want to see you. Would you rather be an orphan who was abandoned in the wilderness by drug traffickers? Maybe sometimes. But for now, try to be patient with the people who love you.

MAKE IT EASIER ON YOURSELF

Going home for the holidays is often stressful because of the intense amount of family time you're suddenly dealing with. Do what you need to do to make it easier on yourself. If you can afford it, rent a hotel room or an apartment for your time there. Tell your parents that you have work to do and you need the peace and quiet of your own place. Or take the opportunity to stay with an old friend. If you live in the same city as your family, find a compromise that will work for everyone. Try seeing your parents for lunch every couple weeks instead of going to every family activity. If there is a specific person in your family who you really can't stand, tell your parents you won't go to any event at which that person will be in attendance. It'll be up to your other family members to schedule time with you if they want to see you.

LET IT BE KNOWN WHEN THERE'S SOMETHING WRONG

Dealing with your family can be difficult when they constantly sweep difficult issues under the rug instead of dealing with them directly. Claire didn't want to bring up her parents' imminent divorce during Christmas dinner because it was fresher than the turkey they were eating. However, pretending nothing was wrong didn't work either. Even if it feels uncomfortable, talking about a problem can be easier than ignoring it. Sometimes there's a part of your life that you hate discussing with your family. Maybe it's what you do for a living, the fact that you're gay, or your persistent bedwetting problem. You can deflect comments and ignore questions, or you can be honest about how much it bothers you.

BAD: *I don't want to talk about my job.*
GOOD: *Dad, I've explained to you countless times why I like my job. I'm not going to change my mind about it, and I'm not going to come to dinner anymore if you keep bringing it up.*

SWITCH THINGS UP

If you're having a hard time getting through family-related situations rationally, you can try turning the tables so you're the one interrogating them. Start the conversation with a subject you know your family members will be uncomfortable with so you can manage the flow of conversation. When they ask you a question you don't want to answer, ask them how they feel about the subject first. If it's something they feel passionate about, they might get so involved in ranting that they'll forget you never answered.

In the months that followed Claire's parents' divorce, family members kept asking her how she felt about it. She thought it was obvious that she was upset and found their question stupid. When she started asking them how they felt about it before she answered, she was surprised by their response. Many felt guilty for not picking up on the signs and wished they knew how to be there for her parents. Others were just trying to let Claire know that they would listen if she wanted to talk. We often misinterpret a well-intentioned question when we feel emotional about a topic.

While you probably feel like you have to attend certain family functions, it's also important not to always succumb to the pressure. You should spend time with the family members that you love, not the ones you feel obligated to see simply because you share DNA. Pick and choose what events you feel comfortable attending and make a polite exit when the situation becomes too much for you.

GETTING YOUR PARENTS OFF YOUR BACK

Parents: we can't live without them, because we would never have been born. But living with them isn't easy either. Some call once in awhile to see how your life is going. Others act as if you were still attached by an umbilical cord. Find a balance at which everyone wins.

One fine summer day, Tessa developed a bladder infection. All the cranberry juice in the world wouldn't stop her constant need to pee, so she went to the nearest urgent care to get some medicine. An inexperienced doctor sent her home with too many pills. The side effects led to projectile vomiting, a yeast infection, and eventually, anal shedding. This, she learned, happens when a yeast infection spreads to one's anus. Tessa's mom, Jasmine, found her in the john when she called. She was understandably concerned, and wanted to be involved even though she lived in Europe. She walked all over Athens, telling her friends about her daughter in LA who had to pee every two minutes.

Tessa got calls from all the Greeks in California. They'd heard about her vaginal issues and wanted to help. Even once Tessa's genitals were on a path to normalcy, the phone kept ringing. Her mom wanted to make sure Tessa had options if this happened again or if she decided to marry one of the handsome doctors who had been picked for her. While Tessa's mom was well intentioned, she involved too many people in Tessa's private matter. At a certain point, Tessa had to make it clear that she could take care of her own crotch.

KNOW WHAT YOU'RE DEALING WITH

If your parents care about you, they will worry and second-guess some of your decisions, even if they don't say anything. Their level of involvement may also change based on their culture. For Tessa's mom, who still lived in Greece, it seemed normal to help fix Tessa's health problems, worry about her financial situation, and find her a husband. If you come from a culture that has a certain expectation of parental involvement, prepare yourself, as they may not go away.

Start by telling your parents how much you appreciate them and how important they are to you. This will help lead to the conversation about them being less involved. Compliment your parents on your upbringing. Remind them that they helped you learn all the things you can now do on your own, and they have to trust that they did a good job. At some point they may feel like they forgot to show you something or taught it to you wrong. You must remind them that they've already done their job, and that they have to trust the foundation they laid. Have compassion throughout this conversation; remember that your parents just want to be a part of your life.

PROVE THAT YOU CAN TAKE CARE OF YOURSELF

Once you enter the workforce, it often takes a little while for you to find your ideal job. In the meantime, you might get paid a terrible salary, juggle a few part-time jobs, or decide to go back to school. It's normal for your parents to be concerned during the months or years this takes. They put a lot of work into who you are and want you to be the best that you can be. After college, Tessa's mom called her three times a week, each time asking if she'd found a good job or a husband yet. While you can explain that constant interrogation is stressful, you can't completely shut your parents out, unless you're prepared to alienate them.

If your parents are concerned for you financially, you should explain your plan for self-sufficiency. Just because you know how you plan to pay your rent each month doesn't mean they do. Perhaps you know that taking an internship will lead to a salaried position or that the classes you're paying for will help you get a promotion. Whatever it is, tell your parents what your future plans and goals are and how what you're doing now will help you achieve that. The more information you share, the more comfortable your parents will feel, and they may cut down on those nagging questions.

If you still rely on your parents to pay for your car, rent, or phone bill, it's normal for them to probe because you haven't achieved financial independence. Proving that you can actually handle these responsibilities on your own without going into debt will help them trust you. If they continue to bug you after this, you'll have to be firm about what you want. Make it clear that a touchy subject like your chosen career or your kids' education will only be discussed if they can do it without being patronizing.

WHEN YOU LIVE AT HOME

If you still live at home, you are inherently dependent on your folks. Whether they pay for all your expenses or just give you an affordable place to crash, you rely on them for financial support. If you're an adult, they may give you a certain level of autonomy, but you'll have to deal with their involvement in your life because you live in their house. If you want to move out but can't yet afford your own place, you can have a talk about the level of independence you'd like to have and try to reach a compromise. Even if you're old enough to get drunk and have sex with whomever you want (at least in theory), it's your parents' right to ask you not to do those things in their house. That doesn't mean you need to listen to everything they have to say about your job, boyfriend, or bedtime. Part of becoming an adult is learning to make your own choices and asserting your independence. Be polite and respectful when you articulate what you want, and make sure you don't jeopardize your free tuition or room and board by offending your parents. Find a way to deal with your parents' expectations for a little while, or figure out a realistic plan to move out.

Unless you're an orphan, your parents are probably going to be involved in your life long after you grow up. Appreciate that they are interested in what you do, and be communicative about what works and doesn't work in your relationship.

ASKING YOUR PARENTS FOR HELP

We ask our parents for things our whole lives. Whether you want a cupcake or a down payment on a house, how you ask has a lot to do with the outcome.

Chlora loved her parents almost as much as she loved sex. Because of a heart condition she acquired at birth, she knew she could die at any moment and planned her departure ahead of time. Her dream was to be immortalized in a fireworks display over the San Francisco Bay. While writing her will, she called her parents to ask them for a favor. Upon her death, she wanted them to cremate her and bring her to an establishment called Heaven's Above Fireworks, which specialized in converting human remains into pyrotechnics. They would then invite her friends to watch her explode in a display appropriately named "Go Out with a Bang." She told this to her mother and father very casually, with no preamble or explanation as to why it was important to her. They felt uncomfortable discussing her death and asked her to drop the subject.

As a result, when Chlora suddenly passed during sexual intercourse, her roommate Claire had to take care of the proceedings. When Chlora's parents received the invitation to her explosive memorial service, they realized their daughter's last wish was real and they shot it down. Had they all sat down and engaged in a mature conversation about the subject, Chlora's parents could have been the ones to pick the shapes into which their daughter was eventually blown up.

MAKE IT FUN FOR EVERYONE

When adults ask their parents for a favor, it's usually more along the lines of borrowing the car or babysitting the grandkids. You might feel like a nuisance when calling on them for things like this, but it's likely your parents will enjoy the involvement. When you leave the nest, your parents have to adapt to spending less time with you. If your request allows them to see you and give you a helping hand, it will make them feel like they're a part of your life again. For instance, if you ask your parents to babysit while you and your husband go out of town for the weekend, plan time for everyone to have dinner together when you get back. If your dad can fix cars, ask him to show you how to repair yours instead of borrowing money to go to a garage. If you have a healthy relationship with your parents, it's normal for them to be a resource for you, as long as they don't feel taken advantage of.

BE PREPARED

Pick the right moment when you ask for something bigger, like a loan. Plan a time when no one is distracted and you won't have to rush through the conversation. Make it clear that you value your parents' help and that you're serious about paying them back. Just like a bank or an investor would want to know how you plan on spending his money, your parents have the same right. Specify what you'll be using their resources for, and how and when you'll be repaying the loan. Be reasonable about your expectations: if your parents can barely afford their own mortgage, don't ask them to buy you a house. However, that doesn't mean you should go bankrupt because you didn't want to impose. Have a frank conversation about your needs and their ability to help, and you can probably find a compromise that helps you take a step towards your goal.

PRE-EMPT UNSOLICITED ADVICE

It's probable your request will come with unsolicited advice, and that's something you should expect whenever you ask someone for help. Of course, you don't want to be patronized every time you speak to your parents. When asking for a loan, it helps to outline your entire plan ahead of time. That way you'll be aware of if and when they plan to butt in. You can counter their arguments now instead of once you've already started spending the money. You can also tell them how comfortable you feel with their input. Make sure you only borrow the money if they're okay with the level of involvement you've outlined.

BAD: *Hey, Mom, can I borrow some money to buy a car?*

GOOD: *Hey, Mom, I wanted to run something by you. I have the opportunity to take a new job but it's too far to get to by bus. I was wondering if I could borrow money to buy a used car. Assuming the job goes well, I would pay you back within a year. What do you think?*

In the first example, you don't offer any explanation for why you suddenly need a car. Your mom might assume you want seventy-five thousand dollars for a new convertible. In the second example, you offer a good reason why you need the money, you set a time frame to pay your mom back, and you ask her for her input. You also suggest a used car, which presumably won't cost too much.

Had Chlora Schlotsky gone about her request the same way, she could have shown her parents why she wanted them involved in her memorial service instead of freaking them out with a lot of information all at once. The more prepared you are, and the more intelligently you frame your request, the easier it will be to field your parents' questions and make it clear that you plan to use their resources responsibly—whether you want a car or plan to become a fireworks display.

MANAGING PARENTS
WHO DON'T GET ALONG

Some parents realize months after their child was born that they were never meant to be together. Others hate each other but stay together for years to keep up appearances. Whether your folks see each other every day or every decade, it can be tough to manage parents who don't get along.

Michelle was eccentric. She liked to microwave her socks so they would warm her feet up but always left them in too long, which once caused the microwave to explode. She felt that a day during which she didn't insult anyone was a wasted day. She was once disappointed with the taste of a pot brownie and wrote an extensive marijuana cookbook. When she divorced Claire's dad Frank, they remained on fairly amicable terms, and she could tell that he was looking to date someone. It seemed logical to her to introduce Frank to Patricia, her close friend and colleague. Frank and Patricia really hit it off, and Michelle was happy for their new relationship.

Eventually things got serious and Frank and Patricia decided to move in together. Frank planned to sell the house he still co-owned with Michelle so he could buy a condo with his girlfriend. However, they failed to tell Michelle, and Claire accidentally broke the news to her. When Michelle confronted her ex about not including her in the conversation, he suggested it was none of her business. Claire's mom made up for all her wasted days by unleashing several insults on him. Their relationship became tense, and Claire was often caught between them.

REFUSE TO BE THE MIDDLEMAN

When parents get divorced, the kids often end up being put in the middle. Whether you're in your teens or your mid-forties, this is an uncomfortable position. After a couple breaks it off, it's usually a difficult and stressful time for the whole family. It can be hard to notice that you've become the only communication port for your parents. Claire accidentally made the situation worse by telling her mom the news about Frank and Patricia, then going back to her dad to tell him how her mom had reacted. Both parents were appalled at each other's behavior and shared their criticisms of the other with Claire. Since she didn't have any siblings or other family members to go to, she let this pattern continue for far too long.

When you find yourself in this kind of situation, the first thing to do is clearly tell your folks not to put you in the middle. One of the most common things parents say when they break up is that while they love their kids very much, they just can't be with each other anymore. The last thing they want to do is hurt their children, but they're stressed and upset and don't realize what they're doing. If you point out that their behavior is causing you harm, they'll generally make a greater effort to correct it. You may have to repeat this idea ten or a hundred times, but once they know about the problem, it's easier to point out when it happens. Of course, you might have shitty parents who ignore you. Remove yourself from the conversation when it becomes problematic. Walk out of the room or leave the house if you need to. Refuse to gossip about the other parent.

If you're a teen or young adult who lives at home, this can be a lot to handle. Find a trusted person who will help you protect yourself. Maybe there's an older sibling, aunt, or grandparent who can aid in mediating the situation. While it's no one's official job to manage a couple's tricky divorce, it's easier when you have a little distance. Someone who doesn't live with them and doesn't have to speak to them every day has an advantage. If you don't have someone like that in your life, you should at least find a friend, boyfriend, or guidance counselor to vent to.

SET YOUR BOUNDARIES

If you're an adult with married parents who fight often, don't let them use you as their marriage counselor. Explain to them that it makes you feel uncomfortable when they ask you for advice about how to deal with their love-related issues. There is a difference between telling your mom what you really think of her ambrosia salad and explaining why your dad hates the food she makes. If you still live at home, make it clear when you feel like you're being used in their domestic crises. Tell your parents what makes you uncomfortable and how they can make the situation easier. A lot of parents don't realize they're inappropriately using their child as a shoulder to cry on. It's not that they shouldn't have someone to complain to, it just shouldn't be you.

COMMUNICATE AS BEST YOU CAN

Sometimes parents get divorced, go their separate ways, and never want to speak to each other again. That's all well and nice, but there are situations in which it just won't work. If their child graduates, gives birth, or has a life threatening injury, they'll probably both want to be there. Unfortunately, you'll probably be the person who has to coordinate. In the case of a happy event like the end of college, you have the right to set some ground rules. Presumably your parents are there to support you, not air their dirty laundry. Ask them ahead of time if they'll be able to handle being in the same room without arguing. Make it clear that you want them both to be there, but only if it's peaceful. If one of them feels that the situation is too hard to handle, he or she will have to make the decision to opt out ahead of time.

Often it's hard for everyone to talk because the two parents can't stand to be in the same room. Email can be helpful because it doesn't require any-one to actually talk to one another. If you need to address an issue with your parents or plan an event at which they'll both be present, try sending them a joint email. If they know you're CC'd on the thread, they may try to be more civil for your sake. It's also easier to react when you have time to think things through and type out your response. While there's no guarantee this will go smoothly, if you keep things short and to the point it's likely that all will be able to get their message across without causing a shouting match.

Unless your parents' divorce results in a wonderful friendship, the situation will never be perfect. But if your parents' relationship is affecting your quality of life, it's time for something to change. Your parents are supposed to care for you and not the other way around. When they ask you for some emotional support, that is fair; but when they try to use you as a therapist, that is not.

TALKING TO YOUR PARENTS ABOUT SEX

Nobody likes to think about mom and dad and their potentially vigorous sex life. Nevertheless, no one can avoid a conversation about the birds and the bees with their parents forever. You choose your level of discomfort and can dispel all levels of awkwardness if you just take one, brave step.

Ben figured out his sexuality at a young age. He watched porn and found that he enjoyed both standard varieties of genitalia, so he came to the logical conclusion that he was bisexual. When he told his parents at age thirteen, they weren't sure what to think. Many young gay men take baby steps into homosexuality by claiming they like all the genitals first. Furthermore, at age thirteen, how could he know? At the time of Ben's confession, now-disproven studies suggested that bisexual men didn't even exist. Therefore, his parents didn't know what to believe and couldn't even figure out a place to start the conversation.

After months of near-silence regarding the issue, Ben decided to break it. His parents, sister, aunt, uncle, and cousins all took their grandparents out to dinner one night. They sat around their table, waiting for their food, while Ben waited for a lull in the conversation. The moment he found one, he turned to his grandmother and asked her how she liked to have sex. She gave a few vague answers, mostly surprised by the questions, while Ben watched his parents blush. Eventually his mom chimed in to try to put an end to the conversation, but he wouldn't have it and turned the inquisition over to them. After what amounted to a very uncomfortable dinner for most of the family, he and his parents actually managed to talk about his sexuality. They asked him questions—partly out of a desire for revenge—and a dialogue began.

While Ben continued to bring up sex at the dinner table—mostly for shock value—he eventually matured, learned to approach these conversations in a more gentle and appropriate manner, and openness replaced awkwardness. The biggest conversational taboo between a parent and a child dissolved with practice. Few people ever want to take the first horribly uncomfortable step, but you prevent tons of uncomfortable conversations throughout your life with just one moment of bravery. Just be a little nicer about it than Ben when you do.

RIP OFF THE BAND-AID

Parents dread any sort of sex talk, even beyond that initial birds and bees conversation. While you've probably endured that one already, you can still initiate a discussion about sex at any time. In most cases, the sooner you do it, the better.

When in a relationship, you can use that as a starting point. Tell your parents you want to start an open dialogue about sex because you like your new boyfriend or girlfriend and want to feel like you can come to them if any issues arise. Good parents will love that you want their help on something they probably figured you'd never ask about. If you have parents who find the subject of sex and sexuality uncomfortable, talking about those subjects might require a little work on your part. Depending upon your parent's perspective, talking about sex may put them on the defensive, while a different person might feel an urgent need to supply you with excessive, overprotective information. Conversely, you may also become defensive if you feel like your parents want to suffocate your sex life by becoming too involved and inquisitive. And while you may find it easy to start the conversation, making it productive and ending it on a positive note could prove far more difficult than you initially imagined.

Whenever you can, just rip the Band-Aid off. First of all, you don't need to talk to your parents about sex in the context of a specific relationship. To start, just say this:

I want to talk to you about sex. I know this will probably be an awkward and uncomfortable conversation, but I think we should be able to talk about it so it's not uncomfortable in the future and I feel like I can come to you for help if I ever have any problems.

You can take it in a variety of directions from there, but don't expect your parents to know what to say. You need to prepare yourself to steer the conversation or you may not get much further than your initial request.

ASK THE RIGHT QUESTIONS

Kids generally don't talk to their parents about sex—human history dictates that it happens the other way around. Parents get away with explaining how sex works and, hopefully, how to have it safely. Their children, on the other hand, have no historical template to work from—not even a bad one. Even if your parents divorced or no longer love each other, their age likely denotes that they have a large amount of experiential knowledge or at least a different perspective than yours. Take advantage of that and ask some questions. If you don't have the right ones in mind, start here:

- *Did you ever talk to your parents about sex? How did it happen? What'd they tell you and how did you feel about it?*
- *How long did you wait to have sex?*
- *What was your first time like?*
- *When you were dating, how long did you usually wait before having sex?*

As comfort levels grow, you can start asking these kinds of questions:

- *How did falling in love with Mom/Dad change your sexual relationship with each other?*
- *What was the worst sexual experience you ever had, and how did you deal with it?*
- *What was the best sexual experience you ever had and why?*
- *How did you figure out what you both liked to do in bed? How did you establish good communication?*

And, if you want to take it to Ben's level, you can ask the following:

- *Do you have any sex toys? If you do, how did you end up working them into your sex life without it being weird?*
- *Do either of you have a fetish and, if so, how did you bring it up without causing problems?*
- *Have you ever had sex on drugs, and do you regret it?*

To the uninitiated, these questions probably induce a little bit of nausea—if not a lot. Work your way up, and stop when you feel uncomfortable. If you don't stand to gain any real knowledge from asking certain questions, don't ask them. You also have a right to your privacy—as do your parents—and the ability to set boundaries. You shouldn't lay everything out on the table. Your parents do not need to know the intricate details of your sexploits, and neither do you need to know theirs. You may have seen the inside of your mother's vagina on the way out so many years ago, but you forgot every feature and characteristic for a good reason. Use the parental sex talk as an opportunity to gain comfort and knowledge, not a creepy amount of detail.

PART VII

WORK

You probably spend at least a third of your day at work. When you add in commuting, occasional overtime, and office social events, it often represents the most time-consuming activity in your life. Ideally you do something you love, but that's not always an option. Often the best-case scenario pays your bills and doesn't make you want to kill yourself. Sometimes getting the job is the biggest hurdle. A bad economic climate makes things worse, but job interviews and salary negotiations are never a piece of cake. You go through an enormous amount of work before you even receive your first paycheck for a job that might not even interest you.

Work can suck if you don't like your profession, but it can also suck for lots of other reasons. A horrible boss can make your workplace very unpleasant, especially when he scares or threatens you. One bad coworker can ruin it for everyone by being loud, unreliable, or immature. Some will even go as far as stealing your lunch, dumping their work on you, or refusing to shower.

While you most likely can't fire your boss or replace your colleagues, you can learn to confront them and pre-empt problems without being afraid. Hopefully something good will eventually happen, like a raise or at least a doughnut delivery. In the meantime, you can create a more tolerable environment for yourself and others.

HANDLING AN UNCOMFORTABLE JOB INTERVIEW

Unless you run your own company or live on a farm, you'll probably have to deal with several job interviews in your lifetime. Proving your worth to someone you've never met is a naturally awkward situation, but it can feel worse when something you didn't prepare for happens.

Claire interviewed for a customer-service position with the store's manager, Jocelyn. While she was more than qualified for the job, there were several other applicants and she spent most of the interview trying to field questions like, "How would you make this a better store?" and, "What's your biggest flaw?" Halfway through, Jocelyn got thirsty and grabbed a drink. When she opened the soda, it exploded all over Claire. Jocelyn apologized and tried to wipe Claire up as best she could, but Claire had to sit through the rest of the interview soaked in cola. Despite her shirt looking like the ghost of diarrhea's past, Claire calmly explained how she would handle an angry customer. The next day, Jocelyn called and offered her the job. A boss won't hire you simply because she spilled a crap-colored drink on your ivory silk blouse, but Claire's ability to remain composed through the rest of the interview gave Jocelyn confidence. If you can handle curveballs and unexpected situations in an interview, it will show your potential boss you can handle them in the workplace.

TAKE YOUR TIME

Many people get nervous when they hear a question they didn't prepare for. This is part of the interview process, because your potential employer wants to see how you think on your feet. You can ask for clarification if you don't understand the question, and you can request a moment to think about your answer. You will seem more professional if you take your time to formulate an articulated response, even if it follows an awkward pause. The same thing goes when he asks if you have any questions at the end of the interview. Employers ask that question for your benefit but also as a way of judging you. Having a question or two shows your interest in the company and the job. It may take you a minute to recall everything you discussed in the interview, and taking a moment will only benefit your answer.

BE HONEST

Sometimes a question will feel too personal, or you just won't know the answer. Communicate that to the person who is interviewing you. He may reformulate it in a clearer way or ask why you feel uncomfortable. Clarifying the issue is much better than lying about the answer. A company may also give you an assignment to do during or after the interview. Whether you need to program a website or translate a Syrian terrorist's speech, be honest about what you can handle. You may feel vulnerable when explaining that you don't know if you can complete the task, but you won't have to make up a stupid excuse if you can't do it. Sometimes the company doesn't know how long an assignment should take because it has never had anyone do it before. Asking for more time won't necessarily make you seem unqualified. It's better to put all the cards on the table than to mislead someone.

JUST SAY NO

We often forget that job interviews are also for us to evaluate a company. Just because someone offers you a job doesn't mean you have to take it. If you realize during the interview that you'd hate working there, you have no obligation to stay. It will save everyone a lot of time if you politely explain that you don't think you would fit in and thank him for meeting with you.

Before Claire got her customer-service position, she had several other uncomfortable interviews. One of them was to be a recruiter at a for-profit college. The school put twenty people in a room for a group interview, leaving anyone open for sudden questioning in front of their peers. Several candidates were graduates of the school, and Claire could tell that she didn't have a real chance at the job. However, the group was stuck in a locked room for four hours, and she didn't know how to leave discreetly. She spent most of the afternoon fantasizing about what she was going to cook for dinner instead of telling the employer she wasn't right for the company.

It's hard to know what an interviewer will throw at you. Whether it's food, drinks, or an unexpected question, remaining calm and communicative will go a long way.

NEGOTIATING YOUR SALARY

We like to overvalue ourselves about as much as companies like to undervalue us, and so we have salary negotiations to find a number that both parties can accept. Before you even set foot into an interview, you need to know your realistic price range, or you could end up asking for too much or too little.

After college, Ben started out as a customer-support representative for a tech startup. When he decided to leave, he wanted more money. He applied for jobs as a developer and a designer despite a complete lack of experience. People at his previous job really liked him and so they recommended him anyway. He got great interviews, and companies actually wanted to hire him despite his sparse résumé. When asked about his expected salary, Ben decided to remain overconfident and request $106,000 per year. The first few companies laughed at the ridiculous request but still supplied counter-offers. Surprisingly, one company agreed to the full amount.

YOU DON'T GET SHIT YOU DON'T ASK FOR

Ben got lucky. Most people who ask for a ridiculous amount of money won't get it. That said, when you know your worth and what you need to make, don't undervalue yourself or let a company decide what to pay you. If you want something, ask for it. While most companies laughed at Ben, they still wanted him for the job and came back with lower counter offers. Not all companies will do this and you can lose a potential job by asking for a crazy amount of money, but if you aim high within reason, you'll rarely hurt your chances.

Before you go into an interview, look up online the average salaries for your position in your location. If you want to know about the salary range for a specific job opening, have a friend call on your behalf and ask, so you can acquire that information without the risk of identification. Companies will most likely provide a lower number or range, so don't worry about asking for more. When they want to know the salary you'd like, request an amount just above what you'd consider reasonable. If they pay it, you get a little extra. If not, their lower counter offer may suit you just fine.

SKIP THE BRAVADO

Despite what might happen on television, you don't want to negotiate using intimidating tactics or employing bravado. It has no place in most negotiations and especially not with a company offering you employment. If a company likes you and sees your benefit, they'll do what they can to hire you. When you bring negative tactics to a negotiation, however, you give them a reason to dislike you and not help you out. Instead, become a friend. Friends do favors. Enemies don't, and you don't want to make an enemy out of someone who can give you a job.

SUGGEST ALTERNATIVE BENEFITS

If a company won't pay you what you need but you want the job anyway, ask about alternative benefits. Startups might offer additional stock options because they can afford that more easily. Some companies may allow you to telecommute, provide extra vacation days, allow you to leave early on Fridays, or give you a private office you wouldn't otherwise have. Many people enjoy quality-of-life benefits more than a few extra dollars each month, so don't neglect your alternative options when you can't get the salary you want.

CONFRONTING
A KITCHEN THIEF

We have kitchen thieves among us. They roam the offices, wait for their co-workers to abandon the refrigerator, and then consume their food in one brief, delicious, and selfish act. Thankfully, you can often avoid confrontation when "confronting" a kitchen thief.

Tessa hated her job and loved her delicious, homemade lunches—at least until someone started to steal them. After weeks of frustration, she baked a batch of laxative-laden brownies and shoved a big one in her lunch bag. That afternoon, she heard a scream from her boss's office. Rushing in to check, Tessa saw her boss sitting uncomfortably on a chair. The room reeked of diarrhea. Her boss asked her to fetch a glass of water and call for a doctor to help with her severe stomach cramps. Tessa spent the next forty-five minutes with her boss waiting for the doctor. They tried to pass the time talking about work, attempting to pretend the diarrhea didn't exist while both remained well aware of how it had originated. When you want to stop a food thief, don't use a laxative to get your meal back a few hours later. You might make your boss poop her pants.

TRY AN ANTITHEFT LUNCH BAG

With an antitheft lunch bag you can deter a kitchen thief by displaying seemingly expired food. You'll commonly find these online in joke item stores* and can identify them by their moldy appearance. Of course, no mold actually exists, but the bag makes your food look moldy so others won't want it. The downside? Someone might throw your food away. Instead, buy a reusable lunch bag or box and put a small lock on it. Few food thieves will want to go through the trouble of removing it, if they even have the skill to do so, and you'll send a fairly clear message: I have to lock my food because I don't want someone to steal it.

LEAVE A GUILT-INDUCING NOTE

You don't have to confront a food thief directly, but if you need to send a very clear message, you can leave a note on the fridge (or even on your lunch). Take this one, for example:

> Dear Food Thief,
> I wake up early every day to make my lunch. When I find it missing, I lose half my lunch break going out and getting something new—not to mention my money. I can't afford to pay for two lunches every day on my salary. Please stop stealing my food.
>
> Sincerely,
> Tessa

This note makes a polite request, but it also induces guilt. If you write an angry note to a food thief, he may start to think of you as a jerk and feel justified when pilfering your lunch. Although often illogical, most people find it easier to do bad things to people they don't like. Instead, write a note that explains your circumstances. Feel free to embellish if it helps. Make the food thief feel like he stole a sandwich from a starving child. Make him feel your presence and hurt every time he reaches into the fridge. You might not get the kind of revenge that explosive diarrhea can bring, but as Tessa discovered, sometimes laxatives backfire in multiple ways.

TALK TO YOUR BOSS OR HR DEPARTMENT

In most cases, your boss won't share an identity with the office food thief. Talk to him or her, or take the issue to your human resources (HR) department. While better to exhaust your other options first, if the problem

---

* Perpetual Kid sells anti-theft lunch bags, but you can find them at many other retailers. http://www.perpetualkid.com/anti-theft-lunch-bags.aspx.

continues you have the right to bring up the issue with your company. You have a right to your property, however ephemeral, and you should assert it when needed. Hopefully something as trivial as food theft won't require the force of human resources, but don't forget that it exists to help with this sort of situation when you can't handle it yourself.

CONFRONTING A SMELLY (OR OTHERWISE PROBLEMATIC) CO-WORKER

Your job throws you into a zoo of strangers with different interests, upbringings, and personal problems. To some extent, you must learn to get along and compromise, but certain co-workers like to blow through boundaries with smelly bodies and obnoxious behavior. These people require additional effort.

Marv was a tennis coach with a rotting flesh wound. Due to his constant struggle with obesity, it never healed, and the medicine he took caused an odor reminiscent of roadkill. No one understood how he was able to coach a sport in his condition, but he had a dedicated group of clients who enjoyed his methods. Claire, his employee, worked in the pro shop and could smell him all day, every day. This affected her ability to function. She tried sniffing flavored markers, potpourri, and scented hand cream to counteract the stench, but nothing helped. She sprayed Febreze throughout the shop every morning, but Marv quickly murdered the aroma upon entering the room. After months of nausea, Claire took another job instead of confronting the problem with her boss. To this day, Marv's leg still rots and torments other employees. Had Claire encouraged Marv to pursue better personal hygiene, she could have made the situation bearable for herself and others.

PUT YOURSELF IN HIS SHOES, NO MATTER HOW SMELLY

Whether your coworker smells, makes disruptive noises, or exhibits anger-management issues, bring it up with your boss or your company's HR department. A good boss will deal with the problem and your company may have policies in place to handle your specific concern.

In Claire's case, the smell came from her boss and she didn't work for a company with an HR department, leaving her to deal with the situation on her own. If you find yourself in a similar situation, confront your coworker (or boss) gradually. Talk to him privately, and mention the problem indirectly if you can. For example, Claire could have mentioned the smell to Marv without blaming him for it. If Marv already knew about his odor but didn't realize how it affected his employees, he might have taken the necessary steps to correct the problem. If you smell bad after sweating from exercise, you don't ask everyone you see if you stink. Like you, most people assume their scent doesn't travel or cause problems for others.

Put yourself in the person's shoes and think about how you would want to be told. If someone approached you with an accusation you'd become defensive. If someone made a polite request, however, you'd be more likely to comply. Make the problem yours, not his, and give him an opportunity to help you.

> **DO THIS:** Hey, Dan, I'm having trouble concentrating. Would you mind turning down your music?

Tone matters, too. When making a request, restrain your frustration. Most rational people have a hard time saying no when you approach them kindly and ask for their help.

RESOLVE DIFFICULT SITUATIONS

Sometimes a quick conversation will solve the problem, but other times you will need to do more. In Marv's case, his weight prevented his rotting flesh wound from healing and poor hygiene magnified the stench. Proper exercise and diet could solve these larger problems, but both require motivation. Marv didn't have anyone in his life to help him and needed a support system. While you can choose to help and offer encouragement, don't feel you need to see someone through major life changes. If your company has an HR department, it can provide the necessary support.

In some cases your problematic coworker may not respond well or take any steps towards change. If your boss causes the problem, make it clear that you'll leave if things don't improve. While an ultimatum puts you in a precarious position, if you plan to quit because of your work environment you don't have much to lose. Additionally, if you're a competent worker your boss won't want to fire you because you add value to the company, and terminating an employee costs money.

This talk might lead to an awkward working environment, but time heals all wounds—even rotting flesh wounds.

MANAGING AN OFFICE AFFAIR

Sometimes you kill time at work by thinking about what you want to do that night. Other times you think about who you want to do that night. If you're lucky, there might be someone in your office who fits that description. Even if you know he's single and of the appropriate sexual orientation, it's hard to find out if he likes you without calling attention to it at the office. Play your cards right so no one gets flushed.

Hector was a copywriter who loved trying new food and going to the gym. The combination made him fun and fit so he had an easy time getting the girls he liked. This changed when he started a new job and met Selina. There was instant chemistry between the two of them, but she was ten years older and his supervisor. He didn't want to risk his job or their work relationship. They exchanged their favorite novels and slipped notes inside with their comments on the book. Hector never shared his true feelings for her, worried that she would laugh in his face and tell him he wasn't mature enough for her.

One day he mustered the courage to slip a survey into one of her books. He handwrote several questions like, "What did you think of the war metaphor in Chapter 3?" but also, "Do you have feelings for me?" and, "Would you like to get a drink one night?". A few hours later, Hector received an email from Selina. In it she explained how inappropriate his questions were and wondered how he could possibly have thought a romance between the two could work. Hector sat at his desk in silence, wondering if she had reported him to HR and if he should start packing his things. Five minutes later, he got another email that said "I'm kidding!" Selina was messing with him and had been romantically interested the whole time. They went out for a drink and cleared everything up. While things worked out for Hector, they don't always. Take precaution when thinking about screwing your colleagues.

FIGURE OUT IF YOUR CRUSH IS INTERESTED

There will probably be a lot of work crushes you don't want to pursue. You may know they're not interested, not available, or just not worth it. You may also not want the complications of dating someone you work with. When you meet someone you want to date, try to think ahead a little bit. Do you like this person enough to work with him every day, go out with him, and not get sick of him? Would the two of you be able to remain professional in the workplace? If things went sour, would your former lover turn against you professionally and try to get you fired? It can be tempting to throw caution to the wind and have a one-night stand, but if you haven't done it yet it's probably because the risk is too high. Sleeping with someone you work with isn't the same as meeting someone at a bar, and if you value your job, it's not a decision you should make lightly.

Before you mix business and pleasure, try to gauge if your coworker has any interest in you. Start by asking him to lunch or to a party with other work people. Once you know he likes you as a human, ask him out on a date without saying it's a date. If he's not into it, he can say no without overtly rejecting you. If he is, you can make a move at a safe distance from the office or at least talk about your feelings for each other.

SEE HOW IT GOES

Every office is different. At Hector's, it was okay for his relationship with Selina to be out in the open and for his boss to make jokes about it. At Tessa's more conservative office, anyone who was discovered to be in a relationship was automatically fired. If they brought it up with HR before anyone found out, one half of the couple would be transferred to an office in another building. Even if you work at a more casual office, you don't need to tell your boss the moment you kiss a coworker. Figure out if the relationship is going anywhere before you add the pressure of other people knowing about it. It also helps to subtly find out about your office's policies before you declare the relationship. Hector and Tessa's offices are two very different places to have an office romance, and the rules of the work place will affect how you deal with the situation.

TALK TO HR

Eventually you'll want to disclose your relationship and follow whatever procedures your company has. Whether you need to speak to your boss or HR, the sooner you feel comfortable doing this, the better. Your supervisors will feel better knowing you came to them right away and didn't spend months having a clandestine office affair. The latter may seem exciting, but if you're concerned about your job security you should play it safe and be as open as soon as possible.

While you should be concerned about remaining professional at work, you shouldn't miss out on a great relationship because you're worried about what will happen if it ends. Hector and Selina flirted innocently for months, but it could have been years if Hector hadn't done anything about it. Take a chance on love; just not too big of a chance.

WORKING
WITH DUMB ASSES

It's one thing to share an office with someone you don't like. It's another to have to work on a school project, a fund-raiser, or an office presentation with a person you can't get along with. Whether he's unreliable, lazy, or downright stupid, don't let your partner get away with too much.

Franca dreamed of being a talk-show host so she could discuss her favorite topic: the human condition. She took a film class in college because she thought it would be good for her reel. Claire got paired with her and expected they would split all the technical and creative duties. However, Franca was only interested in being on camera as she pretended to be a TV presenter. This proved difficult, as their assignment was to shoot and edit a music video for a pop song. No matter what Claire suggested, Franca insisted on shooting a series of close-ups of herself against various types of foliage. These, she said, illustrated the human condition.

Franca did not pull her own weight and was highly unreliable. She had her father, an Italian chef, force-feed Claire to distract her from Franca being three hours late to meet her. She told Claire she would meet her to pick up equipment but decided to get a manicure instead. Every time Claire would try to bring up the problem, she would either get a passionate apology from Franca or a mouthful of gnocchi from her dad. It became too late for Claire to request another partner so she finished the job herself to avoid any drama. When the class offered constructive criticism on the project, Franca threw Claire under the bus and blamed her for everything they didn't like. Don't let people take advantage of you just because you're trying to be diplomatic.

DON'T GIVE THEM TOO MANY CHANCES

The first time Franca was late, she apologized profusely and offered Claire a ride home. Claire thought it was a one-time thing and said it was no big deal. Franca took this to mean she could flake out whenever she wanted. You obviously don't need to attack your team partner for one mistake, but if you suspect it might be a difficult collaboration, look out for warning signs. If she often asks to reschedule, tries to reduce her share of the work, or rejects compromise, she may be challenging to work with. Deal with these issues in the beginning instead of trying to fix them later. If a problem does happen down the line, address it as soon as possible. Explain to your teammate that the project is important to you and you want to make sure you both see things the same way. Use this conversation to address any of the problems that have occurred. Involve her in the discussion and ask her if she has any concerns. She might be stupid, but at least you'll appear caring and she'll be more likely to comply with your demands.

TALK ABOUT YOUR NEEDS INSTEAD OF THEIR FAULTS

Bringing up a complaint with a team partner can be uncomfortable because the other person may react negatively, which could impact your relationship and your project. Most people have a hard time with criticism, so phrase yours delicately. Make a list of what you need from her to make the partnership work, and ask for help fulfilling those needs.

> **BAD:** *You don't share your opinion with me, and you do the opposite of the plan we discussed.*
> **GOOD:** *I need you to communicate more so we know we're on the same page.*

BRING IT UP WITH THE PROJECT SUPERVISOR

You should try to talk to your colleague first, but if she responds badly or doesn't solve the problem, you'll have to bring it up with the project's overseer. Whether that's your teacher, boss, or community theater director, dealing with these matters constitutes part of his job. A good supervisor will bring it up with the troublemaker without revealing the source of the complaint. A bad supervisor won't do anything, but at least he'll have a harder time blaming you if the end project doesn't impress them.

In a situation in which there is no supervisor, you may have to end the relationship entirely. For instance, if you start a business with someone who can't handle his share of the work, you should look for a replacement or figure out how to manage things on your own. Weigh the pros and cons of the partnership and decide if your associate is worth the stress. If you care about the person, explain that you don't want to kick him out of your life. Just because you have a hard time working with him doesn't mean you don't like him personally. It may actually be better for your friendship to stop working together.

MANAGING A CRAPPY BOSS

Whether you feel happy at work has a lot to do with your boss. Someone who believes in you and encourages your work style will usually lead you to be more productive. Someone who glares at you, throws things, and makes unreasonable demands will probably make you hate your workplace. Stand up for yourself and don't let your shitty boss ruin your job.

After college, Josephine wanted to become a famous astronomer. Due to the poor job market, she decided to try telemarketing in the meantime. After twenty minutes of training, her boss, Friedrich, left her alone to make her first call. She thought he'd be back with feedback or words of advice, but he had more important things to do. He did not enjoy managing people and worked in his office with the door closed as much as possible. Friedrich acted and looked like a vampire: jet black hair, smooth white skin, and bright red lips. He spent eight to twelve hours a day inside the office without so much as a snack and went out all night.

Friedrich did not speak to Josephine. He would glide by her desk, look at her severely, and ominously sing "Joooooo-se-phiiiiiiiiiiine." When she waited for instructions or criticism, he simply stared at her without blinking and walked away. When she had a question, she'd knock on his door and ask if it was a good time. "It's never a good time, Josephine," was always his response. Josephine lacked the resources she needed to successfully do her job and had to rely on interoffice gossip to find out important information.

Don't let someone intimidate you just because he's your superior.

KNOW YOUR RIGHTS

Josephine didn't understand Friedrich's management style so she wasn't sure how to complain. When your boss makes it difficult for you to work, you have a right to say something. Even if your company doesn't have an HR department, it's required to meet certain federal standards and post those in the break room. Unfortunately, a boss who makes you miserable might penalize you for speaking up. However, if you feel distressed enough to look for a new job, you might as well give it a shot.

BE SPECIFIC

Figure out the details of the problem before you speak to your supervisor. In Josephine's case, there were two main issues. The first was that Friedrich didn't hold daily meetings and only shared information with certain members of the staff, making it difficult for Josephine to know what was going on. He didn't make himself available for questions and got impatient whenever he had to train someone or solve a problem. The second was that he confused Josephine and made her afraid for her job whenever he walked by her desk and glared at her. There is a right and wrong way to approach her problem.

> **BAD:** *Friedrich, you're a weird boss, and I find you scary.*
> **GOOD:** *It's difficult for me to do my job well when I don't have updated information. It would help me if you were available to answer my questions and help me resolve customer issues.*

While the first example is true, it doesn't tell Friedrich what needs to change and makes Josephine seem weak. In the second example, Josephine voices specific concerns and makes it clear that she takes her job seriously. It may help to practice the conversation with a friend so you can figure out a concise, polite way to bring up the problems.

ASK QUESTIONS

Some bosses aren't trying to make you uncomfortable, they just have a different management style than you're used to. By asking questions, you can find out how your boss expects you to perform in order to avoid having him yell at you over it later. You can also ask for clarification when you get a task to make sure you're both on the same page. If you don't like how your boss operates, you can use this opportunity to suggest how to do the work.

TRY THIS: *Do you want me to file the reports the standard way or in this space-saving way I've come up with?*

When your boss asks about the new method, you can take the opportunity to explain why you use it and how it saves space. Giving your supervisor the opportunity to make a decision lets him preserve his authority while letting you do things your way.

FORM AN ALLIANCE

Sometimes talking to your boss or your HR department will solve the problem. It can also make things worse, because your boss now has an additional reason to hate you. There are also cases in which you just can't risk your job security. Finding a colleague or lower-level supervisor you trust can be a big asset.

In Josephine's case, she befriended Marina, who had worked at the telemarketing office for two years. Her sales numbers were already high and Friedrich respected her. He gave her access to different lead pools and shared privileged information with her. Marina served as a liaison between Josephine and Friedrich, and gave her helpful inside details. She was also there for Josephine when Friedrich burst out at her and Josephine thought she was going to get the blood sucked out of her neck.

Sometimes several employees are unhappy with a department head but no one communicates. Pick a few trustworthy coworkers and talk about the issue outside the office. There is strength in numbers, and it will be a lot harder for your boss to fire and replace ten people than just one.

Whether your boss forces you to stay late every day or makes you watch porn with him, you have the right to complain about it. Keep in mind that it costs much less for an administrator to change his demeanor than to fire an employee. You probably spend a good portion of the week at your job, and it will be worth one difficult conversation to improve your time there.

QUITTING YOUR JOB WITHOUT BURNING A BRIDGE

Sometimes you leave a job after years of service, others after a single day in which you had to clean up explosive diarrhea. No matter what the circumstance, the more peaceful your departure, the less problems it will cause everyone.

Tessa temped at CBA, a legal office at which every aspect of the decor was beige. On her first day, she learned that the building where she worked was nicknamed "the place where dreams go to die." Coworkers were not allowed to speak to each other, thank-you emails were banned because they took up too much "space," and staples could only be placed a quarter inch from the corner of any given page. Claire hadn't planned on staying at CBA very long, but her boss, Joyce, really liked her. As Claire was nearing the end of her contract, Joyce called her in to discuss staying at the company longer. She wanted Claire to rethink her goal of being a music journalist so she could devote her life to CBA and earn real, honest money. She had noticed with young people that it was difficult to get them to give up on their dreams, but when they did, they became diligent workers who spent eleven hours a day doing data entry. She only wanted the best for Claire.

Claire took a few days to consider the position Joyce was offering her, but eventually decided to save her soul. She emailed Joyce to give her two weeks notice, but never heard back. When Claire stopped by to say farewell, Joyce welcomed her in with open arms. She was suddenly thrilled that Claire was going to try to get journalism work and told her to dedicate her life to it. Now that Claire had started on this path, she should never look back or let anything get in her way. After several hugs and words of encouragement, Joyce let Claire go, yelling "Follow your dreams!" over and over at the top of her lungs as Claire hurriedly exited the office.

IT'S NOT YOU; IT'S ME

If you've had a good relationship with your supervisor, you might feel like you're abandoning her by taking another position. It's important to remember that it's normal to grow out of a job. If you explain to your current boss that you've found something that you're better suited for or gives you a chance to learn something new, she'll probably congratulate you. Claire told Joyce that she was leaving to focus on the career she'd always wanted. While Joyce was disappointed she hadn't successfully brainwashed Claire, she respected her decision to commit to her dream. If you're concerned about getting a recommendation from your boss or keeping a good relationship with the company, don't mention any of the things you didn't like at your job. Focus on what the new job offers and how it will help you accomplish your goals.

GIVE PLENTY OF NOTICE

Claire used email to give notice because Joyce was always in meetings. When she didn't hear back, she wondered if that meant she hadn't officially quit. Though it can be more awkward, a phone or in-person conversation is usually the way to go. It will give you a chance to explain why you're leaving and answer any questions your boss has about your decision. Plus, your boss might offer a compromise that would suit both of you, like continuing to work for the company one day a week or leaving in thirty days instead of fourteen.

Many companies these days don't actually require you to give two weeks notice, especially if you're a temp like Claire. However, giving your employer time to anticipate your absence and replace you makes a huge difference. It's not your responsibility to make up for your departure, but being accommodating will go a long way in keeping a good relationship with your former employer.

You can also offer to find a replacement or train the next person who will do your job. If you're a good worker and you have a recommendation, she'll probably give that person a shot because she likes you. This gives you a chance to help out a friend and make it easier on your company. Training the next employee may also make a big difference, especially if you're the only one there with your skills.

HOLD BACK YOUR CRITICISMS

If and when you have an exit interview, resist the urge to be too critical. It's fine to explain the things that worked and didn't work about the office, but remaining polite and positive will help preserve your reputation with the company. If you hate your boss and plan on moving to China for the rest of your life, that's another story. But if you want to be able to use your manager as a reference or anticipate ever coming back to work there, it's best to keep your criticisms to a minimum.

The same goes for future job interviews. Badmouthing your employer never looks good, and your potential new boss may very well know your old one. Even if he doesn't, talking about how much you hated your old job won't inspire confidence. Talk about what didn't work for you at the old workplace, and what you're looking for at the new one.

CONCLUSION

You've now read how to handle a large variety of awkward situations, from starting a conversation with someone you like to accidentally taking a shit in his bed (presuming you eventually get there). At some point, you'll face an embarrassing moment. Even if you've read about it, think you're prepared, and believe that you'll know what to do, you will still probably fail. Sorry, but that's how life works.

As much as you can prepare and plan, awkwardness comes from within. You can't just know how to handle it. You have to make mistakes and learn from them. You have to be awkward until you come to terms with it. Just remember: it's mostly in your head. Remind yourself that other people may not even perceive your discomfort. You've probably been in a situation in which you try to respond to a text message or make a phone call, but keep stressing out about how the person will react. At some point you have to put your worry out of your mind or address it directly. You never know what you might encounter.

For example, we recently bought a dining table off of Craigslist and saved about 80 percent off the list price. Upon arriving, the seller led us into her former apartment. Rather than just finding a table inside, we met the new tenant. Naturally, we found her sprawled out on the couch, nude, with a bulldog on her lap. After she put on some clothing, she spilled Kool-Aid on the table, wouldn't help clean up the garbage she left on top of it, and then screamed at us to get out of her apartment. Most people would find this horrifying. When you have practice handling awkward situations, however, you can encounter a fat naked woman on the couch with a bulldog and handle it with grace. We asked a friend to memorialize the event in a painting and now it hangs above the table. We think of her fondly whenever we sit down for a meal.

For our friends and family:
the people this book definitely isn't about.

STERLING
New York

An Imprint of Sterling Publishing
387 Park Avenue South
New York, NY 10016

ISBN 978-1-4549-1164-7

Distributed in Canada by Sterling Publishing
c/o Canadian Manda Group, 165 Dufferin Street
Toronto, Ontario, Canada M6K 3H6
Distributed in the United Kingdom by GMC Distribution Services
Castle Place, 166 High Street, Lewes, East Sussex, England BN7 1XU
Distributed in Australia by Capricorn Link (Australia) Pty. Ltd.
P.O. Box 704, Windsor, NSW 2756, Australia

For information about custom editions, special sales, and premium and
corporate purchases, please contact Sterling Special Sales at
800-805-5489 or specialsales@sterlingpublishing.com.

Manufactured in Canada

2 4 6 8 10 9 7 5 3 1

www.sterlingpublishing.com